FINDING YOUR MIRACLE AMID PAIN

JOURNEYING THROUGH MOURNING TO MORNING

Dr. Lynda Wright Gittens

"Finding Your Miracle Amid Pain: Journeying Through Mourning to Morning" by Dr. Lynda Wright Gittens.

First Edition: September 2021

Editor and Book Cover Designer: Phillipa Haskins, Fiverr

The Illustrators: Alexkatai and Darydashaa, Fiverr

The book cover design represents journeying through the valley of deadness on a not-so-perfect road, but a yellow Lilly bloom in the crack on the road (a miracle). A yellow Lilly symbolizes thankfulness and desire for enjoyment.

The author is available to attend conferences, book clubs, classes, workshops, etc., to speak on the book. Please get in touch with us at www.livingmydestiny2020.com or email info@livingmydestiny2020.com.

Scripture Quote Versions: NIV – New International Version, KJV – King James Version, NASB-New American Standard Bible, ESV -English Standard Version, MSG-Message, CSB-Christian Standard Bible

Book Reviews

"If you are a person who has undergone major life and death illness, you may find guidance through this book. The journaling exercises are extremely helpful in the process of where you are in life and where you are headed. The writer gives information and shines inspiration on your journey through personal mourning to your new morning. The statement, 'I was not suicidal, but there were times I had no desire to wake up. I am glad God denied my desire.' This is a powerful statement on undergoing major life and death illness and finding a pathway to new normal security. I can visualize this book as a tool in group therapy or a training resource as part of a hospital Chaplaincy course."

Brian K. Gaithright, Preacher, Christian, Author of Children Christian Curriculum, Children's Church Volunteer Teacher, Event Designer, and Overseer of Community Gardens

"Dr. Lynda Wright Gittens, author of Finding Your Miracle Amid Pain -Journeying through Mourning to Morning, pours out her heart, mind, and soul into the body of this self-help book. Dr. Gittens' book invites you to remember and identify the lowest to highest points in your life as she shares the lowest to highest points in her life.

Remembering her depression, anxiety, paranoia, anger, hurt, betrayal, loneliness, and other destructive behavior, the author provides a variety of helpful spiritual tools for the reader to utilize to accelerate transformation, the Mourning to Morning Process. These tools include scriptural prayers, prayers and fasting supported by scripture and scriptures on fasting, prayers spoken on healing by Dr. Gittens, specific prayers for specific health conditions for healing, and affirmation scriptures.

Dr. Gittens definitely achieved her purpose in writing this book which is to guide the reader with the help of the Holy Spirit to a clearly defined path toward mental and emotional healing, which will thus lead to physical healing. The author reveals how emotional stress causes physical breakdown, but God, through faith, can provide overall healing.

I know that God can provide overall healing because this actually happened to me. Dr. Lynda Gittens is my lifelong friend. She actually mentioned how she prayed for me using scripture prayer for healing for digestion problems. I thank God for listening through the Holy Spirit to Dr. Gittens' amazing and sincere prayer and thus granted me physical healing. I thank Dr. Lynda Wright Gittens for her faith that the Holy Spirit would relay her prayer to God Jehovah Rapha."

Jacquelyn Lattimore Knox, Christian, Wife, Mother, Sister, Educator, Survivor, and Friend.

"I didn't want to put this book down. There were a few statements and phrases that inspired me. They were, 'Walk Out of Fear with Faith; Mental Prison of Fears; and It's not your Perfect time, but it will be perfect in God's time.' I will be buying this book to bless a few individuals."

Carol Mitchell McCray, Christian, Mother, Friend, Mentor of Youth, Accountant, and Entrepreneur

Rev. Gwenn Pierre, your shared verbal review of my book and editorial comments were important to me. Thank you.

This book is dedicated to

My children, sisters, and friends for your encouragement and support during my transformation. I love you with my whole being.

My parents, grandparents, and ancestors for introducing Jehovah God, Jesus Christ, and the Holy Spirit to me, which initiated my love and reverence for the Godhead.

My senior pastors, church teachers, seminary professors, and colleagues, for your wisdom and guidance. You provided a platform to expand my knowledge and essence of the scriptures. My seminary's forum provided the learning and experiencing religious differences. Your support intensified my relationship with the Godhead (God, Jesus, and Holy Spirit).

Those who walked with me on my journey to my recovery of joy. Also, to those who desired to be a part of my journey to receiving my joy again. As God told Gideon that he had too many men in his army for the journey, God spoke to me that I had to know that He was The One who made it happen, not my friends.

Those witnesses who shared with me what they saw and experienced on October 15, 2011, the day of my near-death trauma, provided many of those missing pieces to my story puzzle.

My Church Clergy Team members who encouraged me, thank you for including me as a participant in your ministries, programs, conversations, and more.

My Fellow Travelers, on your journey from mourning to morning, I commend you for not giving up moving from trauma to triumph. You may have paused along the way, but you have not given up receiving your joy. I pray that this book provides the guidance you need to receive the joy you desire.

Contents

Preface

A JOURNEY

"Live the life of your dreams: Be brave enough to live the life of your dreams according to your vision and purpose instead of the expectations and opinions of others."

Roy T. Bennett, The Light in the Heart

Have you ever felt overwhelmed, isolated, or alone?
Have you experienced a barrage of negative/crazy thoughts?
Have you experienced grief?
Devastation?
Heart pain?
Betrayal?
I have.

These are emotions most people have experienced. I have experienced depression, anxiety, paranoia, anger, hurt, betrayal, loneliness, and many other negatives, hurtful, and self-destructive emotions. At times, my numerous past experiences gamut painful past emotions.

Life's disappointments, tragedies, deaths, and challenges trigger pain, hurt, sorrow, and grief. I've experienced it all! What about you? If you experience it all, as well, then you know or aware that it's hard to know when one emotion ends or another begins. Sometimes, you are overwhelmed by it all. I was never suicidal, but there were times I had no desire to wake up. I am glad God denied my desire! He knew my future - Thank you, Lord! In those times of deep depression, our response to those emotions can be healthy or unhealthy, and we need to have the necessary tools to help navigate us through those low times.

Pain hurts! Whether it's for a short time or a long time, it hurts! Pain has no respect for a person's ethnicity, gender, or social status. Pain doesn't care if you are a Christian, Jew, Muslim, Hindu, or of any other religious affiliation. Pain is an equal opportunist. We all will experience some part of pain in our life journey. What makes the difference is how we respond to the pain.

Throughout my journey, reading scriptures and listening to uplifting Christian music was my antidepressant vaccine. There is one chapter in the Bible that I had read many times, but one of the verses ministered differently to me during one reading. The word *'through'* resonated with me during that time in a way it never had before. It was especially helpful to me and reminded me that I need to keep moving through my valleys. Psalm 23:4 (ASV) reads, "Even though I walk *through* the valley of the shadow of death, I fear no evil, for you are with me, your rod and your staff, they comfort me." The Lord Is My Shepherd scripture offers us specific advice. The Psalmist, David, said, "I walk ***through*** the valley," not "I stand," "I lay," "I stopped," or "I stay" in the valley. That means no matter how hard life gets; we must keep moving forward.

The Psalmist said further, "...fear no evil, for you are with me...they comfort me." We should also say those words. This verse tells us that God is always with us, leading, guiding, protecting, comforting, and providing for us, and we should not be fearful of being alone because as long as we know Jesus, we are never truly alone. We may *feel* alone, unloved, or even overwhelmed, but these feelings can sometimes be detrimental to our joy and happiness. Despite this, we must make every effort to move through our feelings without stewing on them to the point where they drag us down, and we get stuck in them.

There are times you may feel like God doesn't care. We've all been there. I believe God knows our emotions, He cares about us, and He provides for our protection--protection from our destruction and protection from Satan's messengers. The Apostle Paul spoke of one of those messengers of darkness in 2 Corinthians 12:7. He stated that it was a thorn in his side, the taunting of Satan's messenger, but God would not remove. God assured Paul that His Grace was sufficient. Paul fulfilled many assignments and missions, and he overcame many obstacles, struggles, and persecutions. Despite this struggle, Paul accomplished much through faith.

This scripture gave me life at a time when I was trying to work through my revolving door of emotions after a traumatic experience while at the same time trying to establish my non-profit organization. Through the words I read, I realized that my mental battles were Satan's messengers (angels of darkness) trying to destroy me emotionally. They told me that I was not good enough, no one loved me, no one cared about me, I was a loser, and bombarded me with many other harmful messages that affected my common sense and understanding. During my emotional challenge, I knew that "wisdom comes from the LORD, and so do common sense and understanding," according to the scriptures Proverbs 2:6 (CEV). Satan and the negative haters (as you may see them) attacks your strength. Your mind regulates your body. When your mind is attacked or shut down, your body has no pilot. You become fatigued, depressed, and sad, and you lack the energy to take life by the horns. You don't want to move, get out of bed, or socialize. Satan uses this tactic to keep us down. His purpose is to kill us, for us to die!

We all have our journey. Each one of us has experienced pain (mourning) and joy (morning). I share my journey and others' journey in the following chapters, including the journey of people in the Bible. As you move through this book, you will be asked to review, reflect upon, and evaluate your journey. Why? Because that is where the healing process begins, especially your inner healing.

Mourning

Journeying through the mourning process can be stressful. This book addresses the mourning process and the emotional impact it can have on your life. Mourning is not limited to the loss of someone through death, as defined in various dictionaries and resources. One dictionary defines mourning as *the expression of deep sorrow for someone who has died.* This definition needs to be expanded. David, in Psalm 43:2 (NIV) and 24:9 (NIV), said, "Why must I go about mourning, oppressed by the enemy?" He was mourning not because someone had died but because of his issues with Saul, who wanted to kill him. This verse supports my belief that mourning is not limited to the death of someone we love.

Mourning is experiencing hurt because you have lost someone or something important to you. For example, The loss of income, a body part, a relationship, or trust may send you into a tumbling mental fall. We all go through it! The ways we choose to process the loss are significant in our healing and our ability to overcome the adverse effects we experience from the loss. A few of us stay in mourning because we want to hold on to the hurt. That action is damaging to you. It can affect your health. Some of us bury the hurt and do not acknowledge it. That action is dangerous because you know where it's buried. Any action in your life will retrigger that pain, and you will punish a person that had nothing to do with that pain you buried.

I share my mourning season with you in this book while walking with you through your mourning season. Through this process, know that although your family and friends may not always understand your emotional roller coaster ride, remembering their love for you will keep you moving toward healing. God knows what you are experiencing, and He has a plan to help get you through your process of mourning.

Morning

Psalm 30:5 speaks on God's favor lasting a lifetime. Weeping may stay for a night, but rejoicing comes in the morning. You just need to make it through the night (your darkest moments). The length of your nights will vary. It may be God's design to give you time to mature, or you may stay in your night longer because you are unable to move through the pain. To begin experiencing the miracle of joy, you need to address the issues affecting your emotions.

My friends served as my ears and eyes when I traveled through a dark tunnel of negative emotions; they encouraged me and reminded me that God is good, that He loves me, and that He is with me. There was one friend who reached out to me weekly. We were church members, but we became sisters during my trauma process. My faith was not always strong, but it was enough to trust God at the moment. Because of her actions, my faith in God's Grace increased. His grace gave me the strength I needed to move forward.

Why am I sharing my truths? I want to encourage you to begin your journey of releasing your pain and fear to receive peace and victory. I pray that the story of my truth and others' truth help you to develop or strengthen your truth. Throughout the following pages, I will share the facts and miraculous experiences that helped me find myself anew and overcome the darkness in my life.

Throughout this book, you will be asked to write down a few thoughts that have been on your mind recently or those thoughts that occasionally creep in or reappear, causing you frustration, anxiety, fear, pain, or stress. Also, you will be asked to write down the good and great moments that you experience during and after your journey of mourning.

I hope and pray that you begin to open your heart and mind to receive and benefit from what is shared in this book. By no means is it not a fix-all, but it is a start to your healing process towards your journey through mourning to morning.

Dr. Lynda Wright Gittens

Introduction

PURPOSE

"To thy own self be true."

~ Polonius in Hamlet

What is Your Purpose?

Knowing your purpose helps define your identity – **who you are.** The definition of purpose is "the reason for which something is done or created or for which something exists." [1]

Many Christians love to quote the scripture Jeremiah 29:11 (NIV): "'I know the plans I have for you,' declares the Lord." Another scripture quoted often is Jeremiah 1:5 (NIV): "Before I formed you in the womb, I knew you, and before you were born, I consecrated you...." In these scriptures, God spoke specifically to Jeremiah, but Christians have applied these encouraging principles to themselves over the

[1] Oxford dictionary.

ages. These statements give purpose to why Jeremiah was created.

I believe we all were created (born) with a purpose. Some people learn their purpose in their youth, others in their adult life, while some seem never to find it at all.

Understanding your purpose would fill another book on its own, but let me share this: Do you know your purpose? Why were you born? Why do you make the choices you do?

How do you know/discover your purpose? Consider these questions to guide you:

- What is your passion?
- What do you enjoy doing for others as well as yourself?
- What ideas (ambitions) keep reoccurring in your thoughts?

Share your thoughts~

Write your responses to the above questions down and pray (meditate) over them for guidance. Share your response with someone you trust to be honest with you and is wise in their thoughts. If you need more space, continue your thoughts in the self-care journal at the back of this book.

____

____

____

____

____

____

____

____

____

____

Prayer or Prophecy

Our lives are driven by purpose. My father, a preacher, told me when he and my mother had been married for close to four years that he had prayed to God as Hannah prayed to God in the Bible—he wanted a child and prayed about that child's destiny. In the scripture, Hannah prayed to God according to 1 Samuel 1:10-11 (NIV):

> In her deep anguish, Hannah prayed to the

> Lord, weeping bitterly. And she made a vow, saying, "Lord Almighty, if you will only look on your servant's misery and remember me, and not forget your servant but give her a son, then I will give him to the Lord for all the days of his life, and no razor will ever be used on his head."

My father shared a few of his prayers with me throughout my life. For example, "God, if You give me a child, I will give that child back to You."

My father said he took me to church one day, but he could not leave me at the altar. I hope he meant spiritually, not like Jacob and Isaac in the Bible. (God ordered Jacob to take his only son, whom he promised to give him at his old age, and sacrifice him on an altar. The good news is that God interceded before Jacob could begin the act. He was testing Jacob's commitment to him.) As I grew up and showed signs of spiritual development, my father's prayers became more specific:

"God, make her a missionary."

"God, send her to Africa instead of me."

Has someone ever expressed their vision of your purpose or future, whether positive or negative? Your parents, a family member, friend, or someone else? Whoever you are, wherever you're at in your journey, know that perspective was an ingredient in your development. What was the vision spoken? Who said it?

Maybe what was spoken over you was positive and reinforcing. For example, you can become anything you want: the President of the United States, a lawyer, dancer, entrepreneur, doctor, teacher, or mother. But maybe you received negative comments that derailed you or set you on a destructive path. For example, you are not worthy of anything good, or you won't amount to anything.

Share your thoughts~

Take a moment to remember those comments, positive or negative. Write them down in the space below. If you need more space, continue in the self-care journal at the back of this book.

____

____

____

____

____

My Response to My Purpose

Growing up, I was always drawn to God. I had this inner love for Jesus, but I suppressed some of that passion when telling others about God even though I served in the church institution from childhood through adulthood. I was an awkward child, and I had to develop a hard shell to survive a tough school environment. I just wanted to be normal and be accepted by my peers. My middle school years were filled with violence due to overcrowding and students being territorial. Yes, we had gangs. As a teacher's daughter, and one who loved to talk about God, I learned quickly that those attributes or associations were not popular. I learned to befriend those in charge of certain gang groups and suppress who I was internally for self-preservation. I was friendly to them, and if I saw they were struggling academically, I would quietly assist them as not to embarrass them. I believed they saw my respect and that I also showed some tough skin. Thank God it worked! At least, I thought it did. I never shoved God or my faith in a closet. Although I didn't speak about him in that environment, I demonstrated the love of God toward them with my actions. I am sure now as an adult that God had a lot to do with my protection through my parents' prayers over me.

I realized at age 14 that I love arts and crafts. Over a few years, I learned how to knit, crochet, work with ceramics, and sew. In my 20s, I had the desire and talent to plan and decorate for events. My creative ideas expanded to weddings, church events, and parties. I started an event planning business. My passion for the arts was a highlight at church and family events. I did this up into my 60s.

At 17, I received the call from God to raise my life to a higher level. I asked a relative of my best friend, who had a deep relationship with God, how to receive the Holy Spirit. She said, "Ask God." So, I did. I prayed, and I felt the Holy Spirit cover me, but I was not ready to be a preacher—I was in total fear. I had never seen a female preacher, and I figured my pastor would not believe that I had received that calling. I was uncomfortable with facing the negative comments I assumed would come when I professed being called to preach. But deep inside, I knew what God wanted. I had been groomed for it since I was a child. My parents carried me to church with them during the week and weekends. I was and wanted to be involved in many of the activities. I even gathered my dolls for "church" and preached to them as a child.

I shared my encounter with God with my father, and that is when my father began to share more of his prayers to God over his firstborn. However, in spite of my relationship with God and the support of my father, I became adamant that I did not want to be a preacher but a wife with children and a white picket fence. I decided I would give my life to serving God, but not as a preacher, and I did just that. See, I began to believe the lies that Satan was feeding me. I thought I would miss out on a fun life. Besides, who would marry me as a preacher? I had no desire to live like a nun. Of course, it was years before I became a wife, and it was temporary, divorced after only three years. I never did get that white picket fence.

When I was in my 50s, my youngest daughter entered high school, and God (the Holy Spirit) came to me again with that same unction to preach, but I still wasn't ready. I wanted to complete my assignment as a mother to raise my daughter and assist her in achieving her diploma. She needed and deserved my full attention. I spoke to God to remind him that he gave me this child, and I was doing my best to help her survive and be victorious by graduating from high school. When I think back on that conversation, I'm so glad God just shook his head. I continued to serve God as a teacher, mentor, sing in the choir, and many other positions within the church institution, but that calling to preach did not stop niggling at me.

Your Response to Your Purpose

We have the power to choose our road to our destiny. I believe one road is designed with God's covering. The other road is covered with God's Grace and Mercy. How did you respond to those comments about your purpose from others or your spiritual guide? Were they true?

Share your thoughts~

Share this below. If you need more space, continue in the self-care journal at the end of this book.

____

____

____

____

____

____

____

____

My Journey to My Purpose

From age 17 to 55, I experienced many life challenges. I was an unwedded mother at the age of 19. I received my bachelor's degree at 21, moved to my first apartment at 22, and a new city at 23. I was a single mother looking for a Christian husband in the church and many other wrong places. I served God, being an awesome mom, a model employee, and enjoying a sporadic social life. I had several hurtful love relationships, employer challenges, all the while trying to live up to others' expectations. Occasionally, I would be challenged by a barrage of negative or crazy thoughts driving me into self-deception about my worth. I was often brought down by the lie of questioning how much God loved me if the people who wronged me were doing better in life than me. I was revengeful!

My journey continued to include new job positions, marriage, the birth of a new baby, a miscarriage, divorce, financial catastrophe, and persistent weight gain. I chose food and faith as my go-to comforts. I never healthily addressed my emotions. Instead, I would enhance the pain with anger and wait for it to eventually go away, asking the famous question, "Why me?" There were, of course, some joyful moments in between the trials. My greatest consolation was the health and life of my children, immediate family, and close friends.

Then a shift came.

This shift came in 2003, after the death of two of my childhood friends before the age of 50. Then, in 2004, the unexpected death of my mother—which positioned me to take care of my father and maternal grandmother—and then, ten months later, the death of my grandmother. I took on the responsibility of coordinating both funerals because I was the firstborn. Based on scriptural and African traditions, I believed they expected me, as the oldest, to take the responsibility of leading the family. These deaths were the low points in my life and brought me to my knees. Carrying the burdens of responsibility and grief was too much to bear. I didn't allow myself the time to grieve or accept what happened. Instead, I carried heavy thoughts, buried them, and dug them back up. While my mother was in the hospital, finally diagnosed with a blook clot, why hadn't I demanded the nurse connect my Mom to the equipment to monitor her vital signs while waiting for space in ICU? When the nursing home where my grandmother stayed shut down, why did I evacuate with my family and not stay home through the hurricane until I found my grandmother? When we came back to the city, we found her, and she was in the hospital on her death bed.

These events shared above fed my emotions negatively.

- I wondered if I was going to live to reach the age of 50! When I did reach 50, I shouted for joy during the birthday recognition point in the church service. The pastor said, "Well, we have one who is really excited!" He didn't know my journey, or he'd have been shouting with me!

- I was angry when my mother and grandmother died. I felt I should have fought for their rights in the hospital. My mother should have been monitored while waiting for an ICU room. Her blood pressure would have notified the nurses that it was at stroke level. If she had a catheter, she would not have gotten up to go to the bathroom, which I believe assisted the aneurysm in rushing to her heart. In fact, when she first went to the emergency room, she should have stayed for observation.
- My grandmother was lost during the relocation of the residents in the nursing home. It took us days to find her. When we did, she was on her death bed in a hospital. I tried to find her and ensure she was safe before my family and I evacuated. But the thought that I could have done more haunted me for years.

My journey continued. In 2007, God (the Holy Spirit) spoke to me a third time about preaching the word.

This time, He said, "It's time." I knew it was not a request by the tone of His voice, so, without hesitation, I said yes. I remembered the scriptures said God went to Eli three times, and the third call was the last! I told my father and pastor about accepting the call to ministry. My father was excited because his prayers were being fulfilled. My pastor was welcoming to my being part of the clergy team. He was nurturing during my early spiritual walk.

In 2008, I became eligible to retire from my job with 31 years of service. I decided to retire in January 2009, but I retired in October 2008 because God pushed me to retire early. Within two weeks of retiring, I enrolled in a seminary. While studying, I started a nonprofit to assist underserved students and schools by providing school supplies. I believed it was the will of God. I preached at churches and spoke at special church events.

During my first summer semester of seminary, my father was diagnosed with terminal cancer, and he decided he would stay with me since my children were grown and on their own. I welcomed the responsibility of taking care of him, but it was overwhelming to do it while being a full-time student and running a nonprofit. I was the nurses' and doctors' nightmare. All those thoughts of not doing enough for my mother and grandmother came back full force, and I had no idea how to manage them. I was loud and forceful with my opinions. I demanded respect for my father and his wishes.

Amid this new journey, in 2009, I was licensed to preach the Gospel. My father was there to witness my first sermon and receive my License to Preach the Gospel. He was all smiles.

In May 2010, my father died. In May 2011, I received my Master of Divinity degree (MDiv) from the Houston Graduate School of Theology seminary. In October 2011, I experienced a significant, life-changing event that shook my world (which is the ultimate topic of this book). In October 2012, I was ordained into the ministry, which opened many ministry leadership opportunities. In 2019, I received my Doctor of Ministry (DMin) in Leadership and Global Perspective. Pursuing my DMIN opened me to traveling the world. I went to London, Cape Town, and Hong Kong.

At this point, I was "living my life like it was golden," as Jill Scott sings in her famous song. During our happiest of times, we can all relate to this song title. Life is good, things are moving, and we are at peace. It is easy to be positive during the “highs” of life. Of course, we also know that life is not all highs. My journey, like yours, is full of highs and lows. Why am I sharing part of my journey? A portion of this journey, I believe, relates to my significant trauma.

Your Journey to Your Purpose

Throughout your lifetime, you will have many areas of purpose. As I share the story of my most significant lows, think about the lows you are currently facing on your journey. My lows set me up to take my life to greater heights and happiness than ever before. Yours can, too.

Share your thoughts~

Take a minute to review your life's highs and lows. List those that were most impactful in the development of who you are today. If you need more space, continue in the self-care journal at the back of this book.

Life HIGHs:

____

____

____

Life LOWs:

Through all my ups and downs, I passed through the darkness and sadness of ***mourning*** into the ***morning*** of a new life filled with joy. If anything, through your journey, remember that there is purpose in your pain.

Be blessed—it's God's design with His perfect vision.

Chapter One

TRAUMAS

(THE HURT)

"You may not control all the events that happen to you, but you can decide not to be reduced by them."

"We may encounter many defeats, but we must not be defeated."

~Maya Angelou

Trauma (noun) – a deeply distressing or disturbing experience, oxford language; a disordered psychic or behavioral state resulting from severe mental or emotional stress or physical injury. [2]

There are many types of traumas: Health-related, Death of a person or pet, Abuse, Racial, Broken Relationships, etc., and I have experienced each one.

[2] Meridian Website Dictionary.

My Story

In 2011, my life was expanding. I was graduating from seminary, expanding the tutorial services in my nonprofit, and looking forward to the great opportunities that God was bringing my way. One of those opportunities was my ordination. In the middle of my Catechism, 911 was called.

Trauma Day. October 19, 2011

The events of this day profoundly changed my life—the day of my Catechism. In the religious sense, Catechism is a process when a pastoral candidate is seeking ordination and goes before a council board of selected preachers and pastors for an interview—more like an interrogation in some churches. They inquire about who you are, your spiritual worthiness to preach or pastor, how you know God called you to preach, how well you understand their religious dogma, doctrine, belief statement, and more.

I wrestled within myself about doing this Catechism for years. I believed I was anointed, appointed, and ordained by God, and my father agreed with me. However, I knew that to serve in certain positions within a religious affiliation; I must be ordained under the religious guidelines. I continually asked God why I needed to do this before I finally succumbed to proceed with this ordination process. My conclusion was it would be a strong credential when I communicated with pastors about hosting a Bible camp at their church.

A Defining Journey Moment

The day of my Catechism was supposed to be one of the best days of my life. During the Catechism, I began to feel weird; I heard myself wheezing, and my heart started beating fast. In my mind and spirit, I began to talk to God about what was happening with me and saying to God this was not the right time. *I am doing what you asked*, I said to Him.

While I was having this conversation with God in my head, the pastor began explaining the process to me and asked me to speak about my call to ministry. As I started sharing my call with the council, I felt the water rising and an overwhelming feeling I was possibly drowning in my chest. I somehow managed to push through this, and after I shared my call, a council member asked me what scripture God had given me when he called me to the ministry, but I could not answer; I could not breathe.

I began to spit up what I thought was mucus. The pastor asked if we needed to take a break. I requested an allergy pill. They offered me water, but the Holy Spirit[3] spoke to me and said, "No!" Water began to bubble up out of my mouth. I could not control it. A member of the council asked me to lay down, but the Holy Spirit again said, "No!" Confused, I asked them to call 911 because I did not know what was going on. That is the last thing I remember.

I woke up to a woman's voice saying, "I am going to place this tube down your throat, and you will choke." I did and realized it was not a dream. I realized I was in a hospital room. I moved my arms and legs to see if I'd had a stroke. They worked, so no stroke. Thank God!

[3] Some people use "the voice within me" rather than "holy spirit." Use the terms that are comfortable to you.

The Witnesses

After the event, I found out from witnesses who were there during my trauma that I threw up fluid out of my mouth and nose. The pastor had held a bucket for me to throw up into, and he had prayed over me. The EMTs showed up quickly. There appeared to be food particles in what I was throwing up, so the EMTs asked what I ate. I remember none of this. After the throwing up had subsided, the EMTs felt for my pulse and could not get my blood pressure. They used the defibrillator to shock me three times, beginning at 100, then 200, and then 300. A few people said I was fighting the EMTs while trying to save my life; I am unsure when or why that happened. Before the EMTs rolled me out to the ambulance, the pastor and everyone prayed for me. One person at the church said I looked at them as the EMTs carried me out of the building to the ambulance.

I learned that my Emergency Room (ER) experience was traumatic: My vital signs were not stable. The doctors could not get my blood pressure and heart rate to stabilize; they would raise and drop sporadically. I learned that doctors/nurses in the emergency room left other patients in the ER to attend to me to save my life. I do not remember it at all. I have no memory of these events.

As a patient in the hospital, people visited me, speaking about miracles and about me being a success story. A nurse from the ER came to visit me because I was in bad shape when I arrived in ER, but he said I looked much better than he expected. When I came into ER, I had no color, he said. Please note, I am a brown-skinned American—I still wonder how I could have had "no color."

During my hospital stay, I was incubated for two days, pricked three or more times a day for diabetes, underwent daily chest X-rays, had blood drawn from the tubes in my neck, had ultrasounds of my kidneys, and received daily blood thinner shots. After a three-day stay, I was released from the hospital.

Before I left the hospital, I asked the attending doctor what had happened to me. His best guess was that my blood pressure rose very high, and the blood rushing through my heart vessels backed up, causing my heart to beat too fast. My lungs filled with fluid and overflowed. My kidneys were unable to handle the fluid flow and shut down. Then my lungs collapsed. He diagnosed me with Supraventricular Tachycardia (SVT), but my regular cardiologist said it was not. My cardiologist placed me back in the hospital to run tests and found no problem with my heart. He was positive that my heart had not triggered the episode, but he could not determine what had happened, either.

Rewind and Press Play

After that traumatic day, the events replayed in my mind frequently. Remembering, I knew I had studied and prayed in preparation for my Catechism. I was ready to do it! I showered, curled my hair, applied my makeup, and wore my best black suit. I arrived early for my appointment. While in the hospital, I asked one of the ministers who witnessed my event where my clothes were. Her response was, "The EMT cut up your suit and underwear so they could save your life." *My expensive suit?* That was my first thought!

As I replayed this traumatic experience over and over in my mind, I wondered, "Why did He prevent me from completing the process? I was doing what he asked. Was this a major test from God?" Maybe it was to see if I would go through with the process since I complained so much. I had so many questions.

Scriptures –Bible People Experienced

We all go through something. When I go through a significant hardship or challenge, I go to the Bible, searching for individuals who have experienced similar challenges. There are numerous trauma experiences by people in the Bible. I want to see how they reacted, responded, and how God resolved it. My go-to individuals are Job, Joseph, Jacob, Elijah, Jesus, and Paul. I will share their experiences throughout the book.

I'll begin by sharing Job's experience in this chapter because of the magnitude of his loss. It helps to understand that we are not the only ones facing major traumas, and if you read closely, it gives guidance on how to handle the situation.

A Test within the Trauma

There can be no doubt that Job was tested through trauma. Most would say that this was utterly undeserving. The Scriptures tell us in Job 1:1–3 (NIV), *"There once was a man named Job who was blameless—a man of complete integrity. He feared God and stayed away from evil. He had seven sons and three daughters. He owned 7,000 sheep, 3,000 camels, 500 teams of oxen, and 500 female donkeys. He was, in fact, the wealthiest person in that entire area."*

My character is nowhere close to the character of Job, but I do have a compassionate spirit and a heart for helping others. I love God, serve in the church and community, and my family is important to me. I don't think many of us would measure up to Job, but most of us have good morals and values. Let us not forget that along with his impeccable character; he was also rich with assets. Compared to Job, my finances have been way down the value level. There have been many times when my liabilities were of far greater value than my assets.

I share these verses to let you know that social or moral status does not dictate who experiences trouble. God blessed Job with material abundance. Job was a good father who loved his family and prayed for his children. He was a faithful husband and a good friend.

Share your thoughts~

Take a moment to think about how you would describe yourself. For example, would you say you are a good person, compassionate, giving, naive, stubborn, forgiving, unforgiving, or inclined to hold a grudge? Write these thoughts down below. If you need more space, continue in the self-care journal at the back of this book.

____

____

____

____

____

____

____

____

____

____

Let's continue with Job's story, looking at the following Scripture excerpt from Job 1:6-12 (NIV):

> *One day the members of the heavenly court presented themselves before the Lord, and the Accuser, Satan came with them.*
> *The Lord asked Satan Where have you come from?" And Satan answered, "I have been patrolling the earth, watching everything*

> *that's going on." Then the Lord asked Satan, "Have you noticed my servant Job? He is the finest man in all the earth. He is blameless—a man of complete integrity. He fears God and stays away from evil." Satan says, "You have always put a wall of protection around him and his home and his property. You have made him prosper in everything he does. Look how rich he is! But if I take away everything he has, he will surely curse you to your face!" The Lord said, "All right, you may test him. Do whatever you want with everything he possesses, but don't harm him physically."*

Reading this part of Job's story made me seriously ask the question, "So, what I went through was a test?" What about you? I think this is a normal reaction to reading such a story.

Satan came to God, and they discussed the day's activities. God suggested that Satan test Job. Can you imagine? God said Job is blameless and is a man of integrity. He stays away from evil and fears God. Satan says God has given Job protection and property to place him in a rich man's position. God tells Satan that he would allow him to do whatever he wanted to Job's possessions but nothing to his body.

Share your thoughts~

What assets are precious to you? Cars, house, jobs, bank account, family? What does this scripture say to you? What are your thoughts when you read this? If you need more space, continue in your self-care journal at the end of this book.

Reasons for the Trauma

Have you blamed yourself for every bad thing in your life? Maybe you blamed others? Perhaps you blamed God?

These reactions are not always factual, but more often than not, they are emotional. They were planted by things you may have heard or read regarding “why bad things happen to good people.” You are, naturally, trying to find blame for your trauma. Some people are unable to move forward because they don't know who to blame. After a traumatic experience, many people, some with genuine intentions, others not so much, will say to you,

"It's your fault that you are suffering.”

“Bad things happen to good and bad people,” or,

“No good deed goes unpunished."

I struggled with moving forward after my trauma. But the truth is, "It Happened!" and I had choices. So do you. We can stay in the wilderness, wondering what happened, **OR** we can move through the wilderness with a purpose. I'll bring us back to the scripture, Psalm 23—As I walk through the valley, I will fear no evil. You are with me. IMPORTANT! WALK THROUGH! YOU ARE NOT ALONE!

After my trauma, people (church folks/friends) said things like,

"You need to lose weight; you had a heart attack."

"You need to slow down."

"I am getting healthier after what happened to you," or,

"Take better care of yourself."

Even a former seminary classmate laughed and said, "God doesn't want women pastors."

We all will experience some type of trauma in our lives, regardless of who we are, and people will always have comments on our situation. Be careful which of these comments you take on. Just because it is spoken doesn't mean it's true. "Things happen for a reason" may seem like a cliché, but with God, we know this is true. The scripture, Matthew 5:45 (NIV), says, "...He causes his sun to rise on the evil and the good, and sends rain on the righteous and the unrighteous."

When you have been through a traumatic experience, you are not necessarily thinking clearly, and there will be times these comments may sound true, but the following verses say, "Not so." In the book of Job, God and Satan had a conversation, and God offered Job up for the test. I am not saying everything terrible has happened to you or will happen to you is God-caused – NO! I believe that God knows all, and He at times allows some things to happen. He has a plan for victory, which appears in various forms that we can't always understand in our human capacity. Genesis 50:20 says, "You intended to harm me, but God intended it for good to accomplish what is now being done, the saving of many lives." These words are what Joseph said to his brothers. Joseph's story is shared later in this chapter.

Before my trauma, I was on a mission, assigned by God and full of the power of faith that I was the apple of God's eye. My self-talk was all positive. He's got my back! God is proud of me and has guaranteed my success. I worked so hard to finish seminary and execute my nonprofit's mission, and now, this should be the last thing on His list for me to do—getting ordained. And then it all changed in an instant.

Many of us enjoy having our days planned and working on completing our to-do lists. We feel accomplished when we know that everything is going as planned. We dot all our ‘I's’ and cross all our ‘T's.’ You can probably relate. Maybe you were planning to go to an event. You bought an outfit, styled your hair, and got a manicure and pedicure. Then, on the way, you’re stuck in a major traffic jam for an hour. Or maybe you’re the host of an important meeting at work and want to make a good impression. Everything you've been working on is on the computer, and you're good to go. And then it crashes. Whatever your interrupted plans were, it’s frustrating.

Job’s Trauma

Well, Job and his family were enjoying their day, and then, Job 1:13-22 (NIV):

> *One day when Job's sons and daughters were feasting at the oldest brother's house, messengers arrived individually at Job's home with this news: "Your oxen were plowing, with the donkeys feeding beside them, when the Sabeans raided us. They stole all the animals and killed all the farmhands. I am the only one who escaped to tell you."*

While he was still speaking, another messenger arrived with this news: "The fire of God has fallen from heaven and burned up your sheep and all the shepherds. I am the only one who escaped to tell you."

While he was still speaking, a third messenger arrived with this news: "Three bands of Chaldean raiders have stolen your camels and killed your servants. I am the only one who escaped to tell you."

While he was still speaking, another messenger arrived with this news: "Your sons and daughters were feasting, the house collapsed, and all your children are dead. I am the only one who escaped to tell you."

Job stood up and tore his robe in grief. Then he shaved his head and fell to the ground to worship. He said, "I came naked from my mother's womb, and I will be naked when I leave. The Lord gave me what I had, and the Lord has taken it away. Praise the name of the Lord!" In all of this, Job did not sin by blaming God.

WOW, that's a powerful story and a lot to unpack.

Job lost all his material assets and children. In one day. Can you imagine having your plans interrupted in such a significant, devastating way? Maybe you were driving and were in an accident. Maybe your computer crashed, and you lost all your data. Perhaps you were sexually or physically abused by someone or are in an abusive relationship. Maybe you lost a family member or a close friend. These unexpected situations and experiences similar to these brought you pain, undoubtedly shaping your life journey in some way.

The book of Job is one of my go-to books of the Bible when I start having a *pity party*. It reminds me that even the "perfect" people have struggles. After reading that chapter and others, I say, "My troubles are not that bad! Job had everything! And it was all taken from him."

Sometimes in life, things happen back-to-back, and you can't catch your breath! But, in times where everything seems to be going wrong, I always come back to this story and remember that God is faithful, and good things happened to Job at the end of this run of bad events. Why did God offer Job up for this test? The theory is quite simple: He knew Job and trusted him to be faithful throughout. God double-blessed him at the end of this trauma. Why did God bless him double? God told Job to pray for these particular friends who challenged him and God during Job's trauma. God saw that Job was obedient in praying for them. Through it all, Job remained faithful. He never gave up on God. And God had not abandoned him.

Joseph's Trauma

Job is not the only story that I've read when I am frustrated. I also read the scriptures about Joseph's life. Jacob gave Joseph, his favorite son according to his brothers, a coat of many colors. His brothers were overwhelmed with jealousy at the favor Joseph received from their father and annoyed with his reporting their wrongdoings to their father. In retaliation, they threw him in a pit before selling him to the Midianites. The buyers sold him to Potiphar, a wealthy Egyptian. It seemed the favor of God was on him, but he soon ended up in prison. But even in prison, when all seemed lost, God had not forsaken him. Because of his good behavior and the spiritual gifts that he had used in prison, the guards brought Joseph to the King of Egypt (Pharaoh). Joseph gained favor with Pharaoh and became the overseer of the land. During a terrible drought, Joseph's brothers, the very ones that had sold him, were forced to come to the land he had authority over to buy food. Joseph, who had every right to blame and turn away, made a grand gesture by forgiving his brothers and helping them with grain.

There are a lot of details in this story that I have not included in this summary. I suggest that you read it in Genesis chapter 37 and chapters 39 to 47, especially if these issues of family dysfunction are familiar to you. Do you struggle with a dysfunctional relationship with your siblings or family? Or with people you trusted that betrayed you? You see, Joseph had back-to-back trauma and one bad event following another, going from a comfortable life to just plain hell in the blink of an eye. But good things happened to him at the end of this run of bad events. For those who love him, the Lord works all things together for your good, as he promises us in Romans 8:28.

Your Traumatic Experience (The most devastating event in detail)

Have you experienced a traumatic event? What was the trauma? (It does not have to be life-threatening;

trauma can come in many forms—have another look at the definition of trauma at the beginning of the chapter.) This activity may be challenging for some of you, especially if you have not spent time processing the traumas you've faced in your life. It may take some time; it may be an emotional experience—don't rush it.

Share your thoughts~

Please share one or two of your traumatic experiences still affecting you emotionally. If you need more space, continue your thoughts in the self-care journal at the back of this book.

Let's circle back to my experience. I have seen many traumas on the news and heard many through the word-of-mouth news. I have experienced some rough challenges during my own life. I have had close calls, but this event at my Catechism was my first near-death experience that included a hospital stay!

You ask, "Near-death?" Yes! This event was a traumatic experience for me. It took some time to embrace this, accept that this wasn't my fault, and have faith that God did love me and wasn't mad at me. I thank God for his Grace and Mercy! I believe He allowed it to happen for His glory and my purpose. I will expand more on this thought in the Tantrum chapter. I came to this revelation after reading John 9:2-3(NIV), *"His disciples asked him, 'Rabbi, who sinned, this man or his parents, that he was born blind?' 'Neither this man nor his parents sinned,' said Jesus, 'but this happened so that the works of God might be displayed in him.'"* Yet, being human, I still had questions and struggled with His allowing this for several years after the fact.

However, through my healing process, I came to a place of understanding and acceptance that it wasn't all my fault. I can only attest this to my continuous reading of scriptures and books, prayers, listening to Christian/spiritual music, and asking God endless questions. I fully believe I would not have reached this place of healing had I given up on pursuing the things of God. I sought how do I maneuver through this journey. I read the life-changing book by Dodie Osteen.[4] I also saw stories on the news about people who had near-death experiences and survived; and those who did not. After some time, I started to believe that I was blessed.

Scriptures and stories about other trauma helped me focus on the point that it was not because of me. These also made me feel less alone. I am not the only one experiencing traumatic events. So cross that *pity party* off your to-do list and start

[4] Osteen, Dodie. Healed of Cancer. AmazonBooks.com.
I expand on her book during the Transformation Chapter.

building a new framework for your life. Below are some of the stories that helped me on my journey.

Twenty-First Century Trauma

Christopher Reeve.

He played Superman in four movies. He was handsome, strong, a successful actor, and a husband. He had a wonderfully rich life. At the age of 42, in the prime of his life, he had a horse-riding accident that left him a paraplegic. In the years following his accident, Chris and his wife founded the Christopher and Dana Reeve Foundation to promote research on spinal cord injuries. He was instrumental in advocating for stem cell research. Chris could have remained in the wilderness of his trauma. He was a movie star and ended up sidelined, but through it all, he found and served his purpose.
https://www.christopherreeve.org/

Marathon runner - Rebekah Gregory DiMartino.

She incurred catastrophic injuries requiring 35 surgeries when two bombs exploded near the finish line of the Boston Marathon. She had one leg amputated. Two years later, after hard intense work, she ran in the marathon again. She didn't give up. https://www.espn.com/espnw/athletes-life/story/_/id/12305523/meet-boston-marathon-bombing-survivor-lost-leg-became-runner

Bobby Brown.

Singer Bobby Brown lost his ex-wife Whitney Houston, his daughter Bobbi Kristina, and his son Bobby Brown Jr. to drug overdoses. Bobby Sr. himself had addictions to drugs and alcohol. Yet, through his recovery and the death of his daughter, he created the Bobbi Kristina Serenity House in her memory. This organization helps other women affected by domestic violence and drugs. He found and served his purpose.
https://bobbikristinaserenityhouse.org/

John Travolta.

Actor John Travolta lost his 16-year-old son to a seizure, and, years later, his wife of 29 years, to cancer. He said in an interview, "Mourning is something personal. Mourning is individual, and experiencing your own journey is what can lead to healing. The most important thing you can do to help another when they are in mourning is to allow them to live it and not complicate it with yours." He has been focusing on his own healing and allowing himself "enough space" to grieve. He states that it's important to go to a place where you can mourn without any interference. [5]

Tragedy happens to many people. Don't believe those things said by others. For example,

"God's punishing you."

"If you had no bad luck, you'd have no luck at all."

"You're cursed."

"You're unlucky."

These are words with no power. I believed the divinity would fight for me. I was not in this disaster by myself. You are not in this disaster by yourself. You may be physically alone, but you have more support in the spiritual world than you'll ever need. Call on them—the Godhead (God the Father, the Son, and the Holy Spirit).

Sometimes, people think bad things happen to

[5] https://www.yahoo.com/entertainment/john-travolta-mourning-healing-kelly-preston-death-192158597.html

them because they are bad, did something wrong, sinned, are evil, or because God does not love them. That is simply not true. Don't get me wrong on this; some actions/reactions have consequences. That's human nature and government laws. But ALL bad things are not a reflection on you. It is personal because it happened to you, but it does not mean that you caused it in every case. The sun shines on **all** of us, not just some of us. The rain falls on **all** as well. We will **all** have some sunny and cloudy days, but God will be there in the fight with and for you, come rain or shine. Keep your wits about you. God has given us wisdom. He has a purpose and has already planned your victory. Victory may not look the way you want it to, but if you view your circumstances through faith, you just may see it.

Trauma Reflections

I have had several significant incidents in my life in which God protected me, but I did not analyze those experiences until facing recovery from my near-death experience. Here are some of those experiences:

- God protected me during a rape attempt in a college I was attending, bathroom. I was pregnant then, and he walked out of the women's bathroom stall with a chain. I never talked so much to convince someone not to hurt me.

- God protected me when the brakes on my car failed as I was headed toward the bayou. The curb stopped the car from going into the bayou. God stopped the vehicle headed toward us as we were in the middle of the road. An elderly woman drove it.
- God protected me from being injured severely when I hit a car turning in front of me illegally. It was a head-on collision. I had to go to the ER.
- God protected my daughter and me when a drunk driver hit us in my car from the back. My daughter was talking to me, and I realized she was not wearing her seat belt. I told her to buckle up, and almost as soon as she did, we were hit. My seat broke, and I fell backward while my car traveled down the five-lane highway because my foot was still on the pedal. We did not hit anyone or the concrete barrier. God protected us. According to the ER, my daughter could have been severely injured, and I could have been paralyzed.

Share your thoughts~

Reflect on your victories!

What traumatic events have you overcome? Was there a situation that could have been worse, but God? What are some situations where you have had a victory? Reflect on your accomplishments.

Please write them below, whether large or small. If you need more space, continue in the self-care journal at the end of this book.

____

____

____

____

____

____

____

Before we go forward,

When you write down your experiences, it helps you address the issues, challenges, and pain that come with them. It also enables you to recognize and remember how far you have come from the initial trauma or that you still have a journey toward victory. I am not a journaling person, but I did record this specific event in my life to remember my emotions, reactions, actions, and how much I have changed.

Please, if you have not recorded your experience(s) already, do it now so you can see how far you have come, how much you have grown, and how strong you are. It is great therapy. Thank you for following along with these assignments!

LET'S BREATHE

This chapter was personal, powerful, and pain pressing. Let's take time to breathe and relax our emotions. Close your eyes to pause your thoughts for the count of 15 seconds unless you need more time. Repeat this:

"I am worthy of peace, joy, and a blessed future. I have faced the pain that kept showing up in my present. I am in God's hands. Whatever evil that caused me the pain will not overcome my mind. What was meant for evil, God will turn that pain for my benefit. I am more than a conqueror. God is my strength during my weakest moments; therefore, I am strong. I will no longer allow my hurtful past to overcome my mind. My past pains are resolving, and I receive my peace."

Chapter Two

TREMORS

(THE PAIN)

"Why is this happening again?"

People use the word tremor when the intensity of an earthquake is smaller, and the effects are limited to trembling and shaking of the earth.[6]

After my near-death experience in October 2011, many thoughts raced through my head. I wrestled with the question of what I had done to deserve having this happen to me. The good church folks encouraged my thoughts. Others would say,

"Watch what you eat."

"Listen, you need to lose weight."

"You had a heart attack."

All of these voices left me so confused that I

[6] Tremor. https://www.differencebetween.com/difference-between-earthquake-and-vs-tremor/

became paranoid and started having panic attacks. Those thoughts took off because the medical professionals had no diagnosis of my trauma. My symptoms were inconclusive, and the cause could not be determined. This information left my body and brain reeling in the unknown. My cardiologist and electrophysiologist tried to recreate the trauma in a safe hospital environment but could not replicate it. They both said they had no idea what had happened but could say with certainty that it was not related to my heart.

I was terrified after I left the hospital the first time. The thought that it could happen again plagued me. Then, I experienced a tremor—an aftershock! I was back in the hospital less than thirty days later due to a high blood pressure rate. My episode could return, and I may not live through it the next time. I explain this event in my journal entry below:

Journal Entry, November 2011

One night I was feeling uncomfortable. I checked my blood pressure and realized it was high. I began my usual ritual by drinking apple cider vinegar and water potion. Then I took another dose of my blood pressure medicine. The pressure came down but went back up. The bottom number was over 150. NOT

GOOD. I woke my daughter, and she called 911. Well, while at the hospital, my blood pressure rose to stroke level. Thank God the pressure machine had a chime on it to alarm you that something is wrong. I asked my daughter to get the nurse. Well, that led to another overnight stay in the hospital.

After the second hospitalization, I decided to take matters into my own hands. I made an appointment with a pulmonologist. During our consultation, the doctor shared her review of my X-Rays. She said, "How did you survive? You are a miracle. You had fifteen minutes to live after your lungs filled up!"

I must admit that I was shocked! My response was, "I do not know, I do not remember what happened after I said, 'Call 911.'" I began sharing facts with her about the event: ministers surrounded me during my Catechism. The fire station was across the street, and that we were less than fifteen minutes away from the medical center.

"You are a miracle," the pulmonologist responded. "You should not be here. You must tell your story." (This conversation was the initial spark of the book you now hold in your hands.)

At that moment, my mind began to work overtime.

For the first time, I realized that I was looking at the whole experience wrong. I thought this was all about me. I prayed about the trauma again, read scriptures, and listened to my music. I realized that I don't remember what happened after I asked for 911 to be called. I only remember waking up in my room in Cardiology Critical Intensive Care. God had me realize that I don't know because what happened during those moments was for those who witnessed my trauma experience. I was a vessel God used to strengthen faith and provide confirmation. My being a vessel was confirmed when people shared how it affected them. A few comments,

- Many church members began a healthier regime.
- A minister who stayed by my side from the initial trauma event through the emergency event realized her purpose was to be a Chaplain at a hospital.
- Some people had been praying to God about their own healing, and God's protection of me during my trauma strengthened their faith.

The report by the pulmonologist raised my anxiety off the charts—the very opposite of what I had intended- answers. I became afraid to leave the house just in case I might crash again. I was scared to stay home because the ambulance got lost finding my house the last time, and maybe, just maybe, my fifteen minutes of life-saving opportunity would fail. It was not a way to live.

I was paranoid. I had panic attacks and anxiety. I lived in daily fear. What was God going to allow next?! I did not know if I was mentally strong enough to survive the next episode. Would there even be one? Should I get on pills to help with my fears? Thank God, I realized that being on medications can alter your thoughts and become addicted. I had enough problems with overeating, and I didn't need another addiction.

So, instead, I read scriptures and prayed, seeking wisdom and comfort. I sent out an SOS text to prayer warriors and my pastor, asking them to pray for me through these panic attacks. I referred to my episode as Post Traumatic Syndrome Disorder (PTSD). I kept focusing on 2 Corinthians 12:7-9 (NIV), where Apostle Paul said, "I was given a thorn in my flesh, a messenger of Satan, to torment me. Three times I pleaded with the Lord to take it away from me. But he said to me, 'My grace is sufficient for you, for my power is made perfect in weakness.'" I say to you, God's Grace was sufficient, overall.

A Teachable Moment

There are many times you and I have prayed, wished, or hoped for things to change in our lives. Sometimes the change doesn't happen, at times in the way we desired. The truth is, we change on the inside. We have become wiser, stronger, sensitive, trusting, and growing daily. As I shared above, when I changed my view on my trauma, I saw how my experience helped many people, and it helped me to understand that God loves and protects me. I'm not saying everything is the way we want it, but we must look at our setbacks differently. For example: What are the good things about my situation? How can it be better in a different way than I planned? Maybe that change wasn't the best for me? Remember, God's working on your behalf. It's not in your perfect time but know it will be perfect in His time.

Job's Trauma

As I was trying to analyze why I ended up in the hospital twice, I returned to the Book of Job. Job

2:1-10 (NIV) says,

> *Again, the members of the heavenly court presented themselves before the Lord, and the Accuser, Satan, came with them. God asked him about Job again. Satan replied to the Lord, "Skin for skin! A man will give up everything he has to save his life. But reach out and take away his health, and he will surely curse you to your face!" "All right, do with him as you please," the Lord said to Satan. "But spare his life." So, Satan left the Lord's presence, and he struck Job with terrible boils from head to foot. Job's wife said to him, "Are you still trying to maintain your integrity? Curse God and die." But Job replied, "You talk like a foolish woman. Should we accept only good things from the hand of God and never anything bad?" So, in all this, Job said nothing wrong.*

Job was struck again! This time, God allowed Satan to touch his body but not his life. As soon as Job began possibly recuperating from his previous losses, his body was attacked with boils. His wife told him to stop being humble and curse God. His friends were not any better. They had compassion for him but were also concerned for him. Through all this, Job's faith did not waiver. He still spoke up for God.

Well, jiminy cricket, I am not the only one with back-to-back trauma or challenges, and neither are you. I will admit that I did not immediately have the same response as Job. If anything, this scripture should let you know that you are not unique in experiencing multiple difficulties or bad luck (as some folks say).

I want to share this part of Job’s story, so we can all understand that we are not the only ones with back-to-back problems, tragedy, etc., in our lives. Let's shut down our pity party. And when we’ve done that, let's have a Champion and Conquerors party. Why? Because God said, we are more than conquerors, Romans 8:37.

Reclaiming My Life

I have learned through this experience that how we process our troubles affects how we survive. After feeling trapped by anxiety and fear, I decided not to be a prisoner in my home. Filled with a sudden burst of confidence, I pulled myself together, got in my car, and drove to the Super Walmart! I explain in my journal entry below.

Journal Entry, November 2011

I went to Walmart to challenge my panic attacks and paranoia. Well, that did not go too well. I entered the store and grabbed a shopping cart. While walking around the store and looking at clothes, I walked in between clothes racks, and I began to feel the area close in. I freaked out, left my basket, and got the hell out of the store.

I shared this experience with my daughter when I was safely back in my home. Her first response was, "Mom, how do you have a panic attack in Walmart? It is a huge store." I promised her that it happened and that I did not know why. She suggested I seek counseling. So, I sought a session with my church counselor. I had so much hurt that it did not end well. I shared with her my confusion about what God wanted me to do. I had done everything he asked me, and now I was confused. What does he want me to do? She suggested that I complete a spiritual gift assessment. I wasn't interested in doing that because I wanted to know why God had allowed this to happen to me and why He saved my life. I wasn't getting any answers from God, so I thought I could get them from the people in ministry. I responded to the counselor respectfully.

At least, I tried. While she left me in her office to get the document, I experienced an anxiety attack. It felt as if the walls were closing in. I began breathing heavy along with trying to look calm. When she came back, I hustled my way out of her office and the building. She was there, ready to go on the journey with me, but I realized that I was not emotionally prepared to talk to anyone. The counselor knows me as strong and one who takes charge. I was a leader in the church and a mentor in the community. I was full of hurt and anger, but I didn't want to appear weak, vulnerable, and out of control, so I didn't return.

Share your emotions~

What do you think about the rough times you have experienced? Have you experienced depression, paranoia, anxiety, living in fear, etc., since then? I have experienced them all after my trauma and tremor events. I was angry that God did not allow me to finish my Catechism.

Do you remember the specific events that birthed your fears, depression, and anxiety? Examine your experiences and journal those that birthed fear and doubt. If you need more space, continue in your self-care journal at the back of this book.

____

____

____

____

____

____

____

LET'S BREATHE

Let's take time to breathe and relax our emotions. Close your eyes to pause your thoughts for the count of 15 seconds unless you need more time. Repeat this:

"I am more than a conqueror. I can do all things through Christ who strengthens me. Every morning that I wake up, it is a new day full of God's mercies. The pain from my past flares up now and then, but I control how I respond to it. I will place this pain on the cross of Jesus daily. I receive my peace."

Chapter Three

TANTRUMS

(THE RESIDUE)

"God, why didn't You allow that interruption to happen after I completed my ORDINATION PROCESS?"

My "Ifs" "What Ifs?" "Why Me's?" and "How longs?"

Tantrums are defined as sudden short periods of angry, unreasonable behavior; uncontrolled outbursts of anger or frustration—typically, a young child's behavior. But plenty of adults do it, too!

Tantrums are often, sorry to say, our way of communicating with God. They are how we fight not to accept a decision or event that was not what we desired. You pout, whine, and complain about your situation. Yes, you! If we're honest with ourselves, we've all done it.

Let's see if any of these examples ring a bell:

- Why did my ex remarry and have a beautiful family while I am still single with no children?
- Why did my parents/spouse/child have to die?
- Why did my loved one get cancer? Why did I get cancer?
- Why have I been unemployed for so many months/years?
- Why am I homeless?
- Why is everyone around me being blessed but not me?

When we focus on these types of questions, we allow our tantrums to become pity parties. They are triggers. When we allow our pity party to go unchecked, we risk falling into a deep depression. We may find ourselves constantly crying, angry at others, or unable to move forward.

In our lives, we may experience a season of "What Ifs." "What if" may be the single biggest timewaster out there. As much as we would like it to be so, there are no accurate answers to that question. This question, at times, can create guilt, remorse, discontentment, and regrets, which guide one to stress and unhappiness. Do not let the "What ifs" consume you.

For example:

- What if I dated...?
- What if I graduated?
- What if I got that job?
- What if I traveled...?
- What if I had chosen my first thought?

When a loved one dies, we sometimes wonder:

- If I had only been there?
- If I only made Him/her go to the doctor?
- If I chose... then...?

When a situation goes wrong, "Ifs" and "What Ifs" bring guilt. They open the door to panic attacks and anxiety. Avoid staying in the "If" and "What If" seasons and focus on the facts! It is normal to react this way after facing a trauma but repeatedly asking this question will keep you in the clutches of depression and in submission to unhealthy thoughts.

I asked these questions over and over.

- What if the episode happened after the exam—would the EMTs have been available?

- What if it happened after the exam—there was a church service that night. Would there have been too much traffic on the property for the ambulance to maneuver?
- What if the ER medical team that worked diligently to save my life had not been available?

Share your thoughts~

What are the Ifs, What Ifs, Why me, and How Longs that you face? What are those things that are lingering in your mind? If you need more space, continue in the self-care journal at the back of this book.

Emotions "My Tantrums"

"Why did you allow this to happen to me?"

I struggled for months, for years, on this question. I believed I was doing what God directed me to do, and in the middle of that, He cut it off! I was unable to complete the assignment that day. How embarrassing it was to become sick at the beginning of the exam. Were my nerves so stressed that I was overcome? I say no, because I have had more intense stressful situations, school final exams, and I didn't physically crash.

"God, could You have at least waited until I finished the process before allowing the attack on my body?" I continued to wonder. "That way, I would have completed the process and would have been ready to be ordained when I recovered. Now I must start over! I did not want to do this anyway, but I did it because I believed You wanted me to."

I struggled with asking, "Why me?" I was doing what God asked of me, even though (to be honest) I did not want to do the Catechism; I did not see the significance of it. Why do I want to sit in a room with folks who do not know me personally and insist on questioning my walk with God? They see the work I do in the church. They have witnessed my work. I even mentored some of their children. I worked side-by-side with a few of them. They know my work; I should not need to provide any explanation.

I wrestled with this in my Spirit for years after my call to ministry. Then I decided to go through with it, and God allowed it to be interrupted! Anger set in quickly over the point that God did not let me finish before my emergency event. I reached out two months after the trauma to discuss the rescheduling of the catechism with my pastor. I emailed the pastor and his administrative assistant, and I received no response. I was already hurt and wondering why he didn't reach out to me first about rescheduling the ordination process. It took several years for me to heal from that question. You ask me why I didn't talk to my pastor about my feelings? I was too hurt about the overall event, and I was afraid that I would not be able to control my emotions and respond disrespectfully and in anger. That action would not be healthy or helpful. Was the pastor required to contact me about the rescheduling of my catechism? No. The rescheduling of the catechism process was my lasting pain. It would not leave! Did God want me to do it? I wanted to hear Him to speak to me about rescheduling. There never was such a response. I released that pain in year 2019. I finally accepted that my ordination in 2012 was sufficient. God's Grace! It's good enough. I share with you my emotions in the following journal entries.

Journal Entry, November 2011

A minister friend asked me, "Did you see the light?" That question added to my anxiety. They said I crashed three times, and the EMTs had to shock me three times. So why did I not see the light? What is wrong with me?

Journal Entry, January 2012

I still struggle with what I am supposed to do in ministry. Was I supposed to contact the Pastor again to reschedule my Catechism? I had reached out once and had no response. A few ministers asked when I was going to be ordained.

People mean well, but they can sure say the darndest things. I was already paranoid, and that question, I did not need. It was just another knife in my life to keep me off balance so I would fail. Keep me from my purpose. Keep me from my family. I was not going to let that happen.

One morning after I showered, I raised my breast in the mirror. I saw the imprint of the paddles on my chest. At that moment, my near-death experience became real. It was no longer a story.

I have served God all my life; why didn't I see the light? I began praying and asking God why I did not see the light. No answer. So, I resorted to researching the internet to determine why I did not see the light (do not judge me). After days of research, I found an answer. It said those who do not see the light in a near-death event were fighting to live. WOW. That resonated with me because a few years before this event, a woman spoke to me (prophesized) and said, "fight for your life." I had no idea what she was referring to, but I remembered those words when I was in the hospital. During my emotional tantrums, I remembered those words again.

As I continued to reflect on how this happened to me and why I remembered:

- In preparation for my Catechism, I began a personal prayer vigil, and during one of those prayers, I told Satan to take his best shot.

- An incident at 7:15 a.m. happened during the Sunday worship service. As they were reading the sick and shut-in list, I heard, "Please pray for the family of Reverend Lynda Wright Gittens. She was rushed to the hospital this morning."[7]
- A few days before my Catechism, I woke up in the middle of the night to the smell of a foul odor coming from my bathroom. I thought maybe the city had put some chemicals in the sewerage. It lasted about three nights.
- On the day of my ordination process, I was nervous. I couldn't find peace. When I arrived at the church, I viewed the boardroom before my time was to begin to calm my nerves. While in that room, I noticed a silhouetted figure on the wall. There was nothing in that room to reflect that shape, but I didn't give it much thought. I shrugged it off and went to sit in the waiting room.

The above incidents helped me realize that my trauma was more than me potentially being sick. God was giving me signs, and I didn't pick up on

[7] I have the gift of visions and dreams of things happening in the past and future. I don't normally see a face or get a name.

them.

- I challenged Satan to a battle. There was nothing he could do to stop me from doing the Will of God!
- The announcement I heard at that early Sunday morning service saying I was rushed to the hospital. It was awkward, and I realize that it was said in my Spirit (my thoughts). No one said that publicly.
- I learned later that the smell of sulfur is related to hell. Revelation 20:9-10 (NIV) says, "And the devil, who deceived them, was thrown into the lake of burning sulfur, where the beast and the false prophet had been thrown. They will be tormented day and night forever and ever."
- The silhouette, I do not know what it was. I now refer to it as the shadow of death.

In other words, I realized and now believe that it was a spiritual warfare setup for me. This discovery helped me to understand that God didn't do it, but He allowed it to happen for His purpose. It was a setback for my comeback!

Sometimes, depression can have you wondering if you will make it through the month, week, day, hour, or even moment. It blinds you. You cannot see past the moment you are experiencing right now. Remember, Apostle Paul spoke on Satan's angel: Their mission is to destroy you. They know your weakness and have no shame in using it against you. Remember, it may not be you but Satan's angels. They do not want you to be successful; they want you weak so that they can control you and rearrange your thinking. But know that God said, “In your weakness, I am strong.”

It appeared to be a great day, and then I had a rough moment, and my mind started derailing. I had been doing well that day, but I had a panic attack. It was as if I was back to square one—starting all over again! I texted out to those I believed would pray for me. I asked them to "Pray RIGHT NOW. I am having a rough moment." Did they pray for me? I do not know, but I asked for backup, and I know God saw my text, my pain, and rescued me out of that moment. I made it to see and live another day, so I kept fighting for my life.

Share your thoughts~

Share a moment or two where you felt like you were spiraling. How did you pause or stop at that moment? If you need more space, continue in the self-care journal at the back of this book.

Tired of the Struggle

It is frustrating to be overwhelmed all the time

about some event or action in your past. It's like it's painted on you, and it won't wash off. Sometimes, it feels like everyone knows and thinks less of you or criticizes you, or feels sorry for you.

Do not get weary! Stay hopeful! Trouble seems like it will never end, but it does. Yes, even when you experience a life-threatening health challenge. Yes, unexpected death or a fatal accident. I was healing and feeling good and then was slapped with another health challenge the next month, yet here I am, writing this book.

Remember, Satan had two conversations with God about Job. First, God suggested Job as the target, but Satan was not allowed to touch him. The second time, Satan could touch Job, but he could not kill him. Joseph's brothers threw him in a pit and then sold him. He was in prison and moved to the palace.

Was what happened to me be the result of a conversation between God and Satan? Was it a test of my faith? I did challenge Satan that one time during my transformation to my new anointed appointment. I told him to take his best shot. What was I thinking? I did not know it would go that way. But if it was Satan, God had my back. There's no denying it. How do I know that? God said to me, "What more do I have to do to let you know I've got you!"

Loss happens for various purposes; I am not referring to death in this paragraph. Maybe the people in our lives are not suitable for our future; perhaps that job was only a step in your journey to aid you to a better job position, or maybe something better is waiting for you. Did God have a conversation with Satan about you? I do not know if God spoke with Satan, but I do know that what evil Satan had planned, God turns it around for our good. Genesis 50:20.

We probably will never know why some things happen in our lives, and others don't. We should not allow this to be our focus. Our focus needs to shift onto how to move forward. How do I get better? Can this trauma be prevented in the future? Can I be proactive to prevent it from occurring again?

Share your thoughts~

The fears of my episode happening again taunted me for a long time. What are you feeling now about your struggles that won't go away? What are your fears? It may not be what happened to you, but someone else? Write them all down here. If you need more space, continue in the self-care journal at the back of this book.

Holiday Emotions

The first holidays after my experience were the worst because I was not at my best. Not even close. I could not cook like I usually do, buy gifts, or just enjoy my family. I was still gripped in the fear that my trauma would repeat. It was especially difficult for me because I was angry at myself for feeling this way.

Journal Entry, December 2011

The holidays are here. I am grateful to see my children, grandchildren, and the whole family. I usually cook the meal, but I was limited to a few dishes because of my mental fatigue. I still battled with, "Why, God?" I am still working through panic attacks, depression, and anxiety.

Tantrums During the Holidays

Holidays and celebrations can be challenging during a tantrum and can arouse painful memories and emotions. How are your holidays? Are you able to enjoy them? Do you shut down, sit quietly, or isolate yourself? Do you attend holiday events? Family gatherings? How do you handle your tantrum during the holidays and other events? Do you experience grief over the loss of someone you loved? Or a job you lost? Or a failure? Or poor self-esteem?

Share your thoughts~

What do you do to help make it through the holidays? Any holiday, birthday, anniversary, etc. If you need more space, continue in the self-care journal at the back of this book.

____

____

____

____

____

____

An AHa Moment

The New Year of 2012 brought no joy but only more mourning. It had been almost two months since my trauma. I still had not seen or heard from God about my ordination process. I didn't want to go back to the council. My irrational fear was that they feared me and a repeat of what happened the first time. Also, the EMTs cut my clothes off. Was that in the meeting room in front of the council, in the ambulance, or the ER? I just didn't know, and I was embarrassed by the thought.

I will admit that my panic attacks and paranoia were improving, and I moved around the city more. I remained a little fearful in the back of my head, but I pushed through it because I didn't want to be trapped in orbit, never to return. It's incredible how the mind works.

I finally received a preview of God's response to one of my questions.

Journal Entry, February 2012

This Sunday service was with a visiting old-school pastor. During his sermon about the 'magi' (wise men) visiting Jesus. He stated that Herod wanted to kill the 'magi', but God sent angels to tell them that he was sending them another way. Those six words spoke to me—"God was sending them another way." Was God sending me another way? Did I no longer need to be ordained? I emotionally broke down and cried loudly like a baby in the sanctuary. I could not stop. Was God answering my prayers through this preacher? I felt so much peace.

Now, what was that way?

That sermon was an "aha" moment for me, as Oprah would say. It gave me hope. I did not know what the details were, but for the first time in a while, I believed that there was a plan for victory and that it would be revealed to me at the right time. I continued to fight for my life, even harder than before. I read scriptures that discussed what I was going through and prayed over them.

I still have questions about my trauma, but I decided to keep moving in the ministry, being observant to new opportunities making themselves available. I decided to put on the Whole Armor of God and be alert; Ephesians 6:11-18.

Journal Entry, July 25, 2012

Where do I go from here, God? Where do I go? I just do not understand why I was prevented from completing my Catechism, what I believed you wanted me to do. You allowed my sickness to happen; I trust you, so I am waiting for your direction.

At the moment of this journal entry, God had not shared His plan, nor had I seen or heard any news about my future. I had no idea what to do. God did not say *go back to the Pastor, reschedule, contact the Pastor, or forget about the Catechism. Go to another Pastor to help with your being ordained because that way, you aren't embarrassed.* What do I do? God, how are you going to make this work? The wait is the hardest. What does one do in the meantime? I prayed, worked, and kept on living until I received direction.

In September, God guided me to learn about the Joan Hunters Ministries. I knew about their ordination program because I had shared it with other ministers who wanted to be ordained. One of the largest churches in my city sends its ministers there. In my review of the program, one of the ministry's purposes was a healing school. I thought that was why God led me to view the ministry again. I meditated on this, and I signed up for the healing classes and the ordination program. I was ordained to the ministry in October 2012.

Share your thoughts~

What question(s) or action(s) are you waiting for an answer on? If you need more space, continue in the self-care journal at the back of this book.

Encouragement

I could no longer linger in pity, although it took me a few years to completely heal from that mental prison of fear of questioning, "Why?"

As time went on, I would compare how I was last month to the current month. Then I would set goals for myself to survive the fears I was still facing. I continued in prayer and setting goals. I continued waiting on God's direction, wisdom, and discernment! I was trying to do it on my own and for my merit. I frustrated myself because it was not going the way I had decided it would. I started a Bible camp at an apartment complex, but the management changed their minds and said no. I was hurt—another shut door. To my amazement, a church sister minister serving the community connected me with another sister minister who had a program in an apartment complex. Look at God! He did want me to host the Bible camps at apartment complexes. I served at that apartment complex (KR) for four years. I began hosting bible camps at other apartment complexes and churches while still hosting at apartment KR.

Journal Entry - August 2012

I am tired of trying to make the mentor/tutor program become a reality. Everywhere I go, the apartment complex management was disrespectful regarding not returning calls. I am struggling to maintain the volunteers. Read some scriptures and heard a pastor speak on "Keep Fighting." Pastor TD Jakes said, "Your passion is your purpose." I worked on the youth programs and my ordination, and then I woke up on a ventilator. I am not going back there again. I am just going to do nothing on the youth program and JUST WAIT!

One positive thing that I chose to focus on was being able to help others during their anxiety after a significant event in their lives. I put to work what I practiced in my own life in helping release myself from those awful "Ifs" and "What Ifs." It was so great to see the joy on their faces and the newfound freedom to live. Through my trauma and difficulties, I was able to help others be free from their pain and emotions.

We put a lot of pressure on ourselves to get things done. To make things happen. We need to learn that not everything is urgent or immediately in need of attention. Psalms 27:14 (NIV) says, "Wait for the Lord; be strong and take heart and wait for the Lord."

"Wait" does not mean to just sit in all cases. God says to be of good courage. Hang in there. Do your best. He will strengthen your heart to keep going. Do not give up! Seek His direction. Deuteronomy 31:6 is one of several verses that make this common statement.

Twenty-First Century Encouragement

Actor Christopher Reeve lost his acting career and his ability to move, but he didn't lose his relationship with actors. He advocated throughout the remainder of his life for stem cell research. He and his wife spent years getting support and grants for stem cell research. He didn't live to benefit physically, but their efforts helped many others because the stem cell procedures are now a reality.

Seven-year-old Megan Kanka, a New Jersey girl who was raped and killed by a known registered sex offender who had moved across the street from the family without their knowledge, was the catalyst for Megan's Law, created to help save children from sexual offenders. In the wake of the tragedy, the Kanka family sought to have local communities warned about sex offenders in the area. All states now have a form of Megan's Law. Her death was a tragedy and beyond painful for her family, but her family fought to help save other children through their grief.

Many wonderful, meaningful things have developed through tragedy. It's hurtful but sometimes necessary to help others. I believe that God sustained me because I had to continue to bring the nonprofit to fruition. I struggled through the creation and development of this nonprofit to help students diagnosed with learning disabilities and students unable to stay after school to receive the academic assistance they need residing in underserved communities. It is now established and functioning.

Share your thoughts~

What good thing has happened out of your trauma? It could be personal, in the community, or public. If you have not yet created or ministered through your trauma, grief, or pain, have you had ideas, thoughts, or visions about doing something? That's possibly *your miracle amid your pain.* If you need more space, continue in the self-care journal at the back of this book.

My Flashback

Let's return to my "What Ifs" mentioned at the beginning of this chapter. I have since received insights into some of my "What Ifs." Some directly from the Holy Spirit.

If God had allowed my trauma to happen at any other time, I might not be alive. He had everything aligned. The location was a room of ministers, across the street from the fire station and a short run to the medical center.

I also realized that some of the bad things in my life were allowed by God, which disturbed me. If I believed God was all-knowing, then God knew the bad things were going to happen. I began to fear God's allowances. If He would allow this significant near-death experience to happen to me, how far would He go? God's response, "What more do I have to do to let you know that I got you?" That quieted my fear and encouraged my faith.

Another revelation for me was realizing that I summoned God's protection through this journey, and He brought me out alive and kicking. He provided for me, blessed me, and gave me favor. I am still here!

A few of you may wish you were in this place of

peace. I say to you, don't let those hateful thoughts overwhelm you. Find a place of tranquility: mentally, spiritually, and physically. Try listening to uplifting music, read uplifting books, poems, scripture, etc. Whatever puts a smile on your face. Do an activity that will bring excitement to you that day, week, month, or in life. Give it a chance. Yes, it's out of your comfort zone, but it's worth it! Just do it!

Yes, my first step was Walmart. No, it didn't go as I hoped. I had no expectations, but I didn't let it deter me. I sat and reviewed what happened, what I was doing, and where I was in that store. I decided to go back and avoid the tight spaces but walk in open areas. Face what I was ready to challenge, and it worked. With each new trip to the store, I felt braver. A miracle amid my pain.

Reflections on My Feelings about My Past Traumas

I have had moments in my life where God allowed me to experience physical abuse. When this happened, I thought He did not love me. I felt betrayed and abandoned. Those incidents shook my relationship with Him, but they did not destroy me.

I did my best to hold on to the fact that God existed. It hurt like hell, but I knew I wasn't the only person on earth who had experienced this. My situation could have been worse. Since then, I have been able to counsel others who have experienced abuse.

Again, I have experienced significant life-threatening events, but God allowed me to walk away without a scratch. God is great!

These days, when I do not hear from God or see a sign, I remember that the teacher is always quiet during the test.

"Jesus was a teacher and a rabbi. God is silent at times because he has poured into us everything; we need to pass the test!!" ~ Pastor Sheryl Brady

---

Share your thoughts~

Take a moment to write down your current emotions about your trauma. Be honest with your thoughts, anger, questions, doubts, etc. If you need more space, continue in the self-care journal at the back of this book.

Moving Forward

It's okay to question why. It's a natural response. But it is not safe to continue to think about it for a lifetime. Some Christians or preachers tell you that you can't question God. That is untrue. God will answer what he determines you need to know. Now I express my anger, and He immediately responds. I'm not saying that's a suitable method, but God knows you are angry. He understands. God ain't scared of you! I kept asking God why he allowed this to happen. He finally responded, "What more do I have to do to show you that I've got you!" I felt a level of His disappointment that I still had so little trust and belief that He loves me. Enough said.

Job Questioned God

"I desire to speak to the Almighty and to argue my case with God," Job said. (Job 12; Job 13:3; Job 9:13-20; Job 23) Job said that his complaint was bitter, it filled his mouth with arguments, and the righteous might dispute with him. However, he does acknowledge the power of God. Job went before God and made his case, and God responded. God asked where he was when the earth's foundation was laid, or the morning stars were placed during creation? God continued, asking Job if he was correcting Him or accusing Him. He asked Job to respond to His questions. Job decided not to talk anymore. This discussion crosses many chapters in the book of Job. The bottom line is that when we have questions of God, we must be respectful in our approach. God is Sovereign, meaning He is the supreme authority and can do whatever He desires. He is our creator, protector, guide, and more. Yet, He allows us to come to Him and express how we feel.

Share your thoughts~

What questions would you want to ask God? What do you want to say? If you need more space, use the self-care journal at the back of the book.

Keep Fighting for your purpose! Don't give up! Read scriptures, meditate, listen to music, whatever gives you peace and strength. Plan, plan, plan. The scriptures say, "Where there is no revelation, people cast off restraint; But blessed is the one who heeds wisdom's instruction." (Proverbs 29:18NIV); and "Then the Lord replied: 'Write down the revelation and make it plain on tablets so that a herald may run with it.'" (Habakkuk 2:2NIV)

You need to share your vision with God. Know that His direction may not be immediate, but it will be for you to move with the vision. God guides you in many ways. If He agrees, you will hear from Him. His response could be through sound/voice, visions, dreams, signs, or other people that set you on the journey and confirm your thoughts. Yes, I shared my vision, the desires of my heart. Yes, I kept working on it. Yes, I'm still working on it, but it's a little easier now.

Share your Plans~

What plans have you created, developed, or pursued? Plans that may or may not have come to pass. If you need more space, continue in the self-care journal at the back of this book.

LET'S BREATHE

Let's take time to breathe and relax our emotions. Close your eyes to pause your thoughts for the count of 15 seconds unless you need more time. Repeat this:

"I embrace my frustration and empower my mind. I will not grow weary but be an eagle of strength. I will not hold in my frustrations but share them with God or my confidant for wisdom. Also, I will listen to their guidance. I will receive peace."

Chapter Four

TRANSFORMATIONS

Journeying through the valley towards joy

Psalm 41:1-3 NASB

How blessed is he who considers the helpless; The LORD will deliver him in a day of trouble. The LORD will protect him and keep him alive, and he shall be called blessed upon the earth; and do not turn him over to the desire of his enemies. The LORD will sustain him upon his sickbed; in his illness, You restored him to health.

Transformation is a thorough or dramatic change in form or appearance, a metamorphosis during the life cycle of an animal. [8]

Metamorphosis is a change of the form or nature of a thing or person into a completely different one by natural or supernatural means. [9]

---

[8] Oxford Language website.

[9] Ibid.

Prayer is a spiritual communication action with God or one object of worship, as in supplication, thanksgiving, adoration, or confession. [10]

Meditation is a set of techniques that are intended to encourage a heightened state of awareness and focused attention. A consciousness change technique has been shown to have a vast number of benefits on psychological well-being. [11]

PURPOSE

Shedding the Dead Skin

I'm sure you've heard of the caterpillar that sheds its skin up to five times during its transformation to become a butterfly.[12] A snake sheds its skin to allow further growth and remove parasites attached to its old skin.[13] In our lives, perhaps we can relate to facials as a process of cleansing, exfoliating, clearing imperfections, and nourishing the skin, promoting a clear, well-hydrated complexion.

---

[10] www.verywellmind.com

[11] Ibid.

[12] www.earthtouchnews.com Timelapse: Watch a caterpillar crawl out of its skin by Andy Jeffery, September 11, 2015

[13] www.wonderopolis.org Why Do Snakes Shed Their Skin?

We have all suffered through painful situations, but who we have become after the pain should be glowing beautifully. Some of us may still be scared, but our inner healing is essential. Once healed on the inside, our body begins to heal on the outside.

Remember, I went through this physical trauma with minor scars on my physical body. My body had the markings of the IV, the incision from the blood tubes in my neck, and the six rectangular markings on my chest from the shock treatment. They disappeared with time, but I had severe internal scars because the trauma had affected my emotions, faith, and trust in God. To survive, I had to work on healing internally.

After a time, I began to hear specific directions from God. He gave me orders to shed my church leadership positions by the year 2012. I didn't understand why at the time, but I knew it was something I needed to follow.

Journal Entry, January 2012

I spent time removing myself from leadership positions in the church, according to God's direction. God told me in 2011 to remove myself from all church leadership positions in 2012. It was an emotional process, but I managed to do it.

Removing Myself from Leadership

Some of those positions God wanted me to retire from were personal and important to me. I had held them for years. One was Girl Scout Leader, which I held over several years. I loved the girls; working with young people was my passion. I let go of all positions but two. I held on to those positions because I didn't hold the lead position. I kept teaching Vacation Bible School (VBS) and secretary position on the Church's African Project Board. The VBS teaching position was one I had held for years and was reluctant to let go. The coordinator asked if I was going to teach this year, and I said yes. I was not in charge of the program. Well, the coordinator did not include me in the communication. I contacted the coordinator two weeks before the start of VBS to see if the books had been distributed or whether there had been a meeting. That's when they realized I was not on the email list. The African Project Board had a long stretch of no meetings; therefore, I reached out to one of the members to see if they were meeting, and he said he hadn't heard anything either. No more board position. God does have a sense of humor, Christians say. I didn't step away from those positions because I did not see them as me being in charge, but God had a different view and removed those positions from me in His way.

Why do we need to transform? Because our grieving, unforgiveness, resentment, rejection, bad decisions, pain, anger, stress, and other negative emotions interfere with our growth.

We need to be purified. We need to clear out that poison that is within us. Some may need a bypass. Some may need stitches. Some may need a transplant. Our internal bodies—mind and heart—need to be purified to grow, shine, have joy, and live again. Sometimes, to transform and let the new in, we need to let go of certain things.

Isaiah 43:19 (NIV) says, "See, I am doing a new thing! Now it springs up; do you not perceive it? I am making a way in the wilderness and streams in the wasteland."

In my own post-trauma life, I had to accept that I

was having or experiencing a mental issue(s). My fears were so intense that I was afraid to sleep because I thought I might not wake up. I was scared to wake up because I was afraid to live. I was afraid to live because I may get sick again and may not make it to the hospital within 15 minutes. It was a vicious cycle for months. I will say, the fear reduced gradually over the years. Now I am healed from that daily fear, and I am free to live. I believe every day is my destiny, and I will live it in peace because God woke me up and designed my journey. I always believed, but now I can honestly say I trust God again.

Have you seen the TV show, Hoarders? You may have noticed that most people on this show have experienced some trauma or loss in their lives. They have closed themselves off from people (including family) by filling their homes with stuff. Their actions have led to roaches, rats, mold, mountains of trash, and rotting food. Trauma can put you in a funk and even severe depression by causing you to stay closed in and closed off from people, life, or new experiences. It is horrible and sad to see good, wonderful, loving people live like this because they can't or won't release the pain and seek life. The hoarding of material stuff is a powerful metaphor for the state of our inner lives if we don't commit to inner healing. We are hoarding painful memories.

Have you seen the show, *My 600lb Life*? Almost without realizing how their actions affected them, they found themselves so large that they are immobile, in pain, facing severe health challenges, imposing on their loved ones and others who have to sacrifice their lives to aid them. Many of these people resort to food for comfort, protection, or love. Emotional eating because of painful memories can and will destroy you.

Check out these stories. I watch them because the stories of these individuals help me to keep myself in check. Many times in my life, I ate based on emotions and not because I was hungry. I worked diligently to acknowledge that I should not eat if I am not hungry and eating out of emotions or habits. It is still a struggle at times. I don't want to be unable to wash my body and have my children take on that responsibility. I want to travel. These severely obese people can't because of their size or immobility. The hoarders can't have their children in their homes because it is unsafe. They lost relationships with their children, family, and friends because they can't let go of the stuff in their homes. Are you living like this? Do you want to live like this?

Do you know people living like this? THERE IS HOPE!!! Begin to create good memories!

These TV shows not only reference their story of pain but of possibilities. They have reached a point in their depression that they do want joy again. They want their children, family, and friends in their lives. So, they reached out for help to a therapist specializing in organization and doctors specializing in weight loss. They have a team of clutter organizers, therapists, psychologists, junk haulers, and more to help them change their lives successfully. THERE IS HOPE!!!

We must understand that transformation is not only physical but mental. Trauma affects the mind as well as the physical body. Sometimes, the physical heal faster than the mind, and vice-versa. I sought and visited specialists after my trauma to determine my health status (body and mind). I was examined, tested, and medicated to help my body recover and strengthen. I sought help for my mental state. I found I could open up to and pray with a sister preacher. I also read the scriptures and prayed. If you are a spiritual person, I strongly suggest finding a counselor or friend, reading the scriptures, and praying. If you are not spiritual, get therapy or find someone with wisdom that cares about your success.

Philippians 3:13-14 tells us to focus on the GOAL! We have to shed what is keeping us bound.

PROCESS

Why is there a need to shed, prune, cut, etc.?

God prunes us according to John 15:1-3 (MSG). Jesus said, "I am the Real Vine, and my Father is the Farmer. He cuts off every branch of me that doesn't have grapes. And every branch that is grape-bearing he prunes back so it will bear even more. You are already pruned back by the message I have spoken."

Philippians 3:12-14 (MSG) said, "I'm not saying that I have this all together, that I have it made. But I am well on my way, reaching out for Christ, who has so wondrously reached out for me. Friends, don't get me wrong: By no means do I count myself an expert in all of this, but I've got my eye on the goal, where God is beckoning us onward—to Jesus. I'm off and running, and I'm not turning back."

These verses above speak on Spiritual pruning.

"Spiritual pruning enhances spiritual growth by removing whatever inhibits spiritual growth." [14] The process can be painful because of "our reluctance to give up whatever inhibits our growth. For example, habits, attitudes and thoughts." [15] Our pruning may include isolation, changes in relationships, being drawn closer to God due to uncomfortable circumstances, being placed in positions outside our comfort zone, and other actions.

Jonah's Transformation

Do you know this story? Jonah refused to do what God wanted. He had his own opinion about the people in Nineveh. In fact, he argued with God and decided to go his own way. He was on a boat, running away, and a storm came. Jonah took the blame as the cause of the storm, and he was thrown over the boat into the water, and the storm stopped. A large fish swallowed Jonah. While he was confined in the belly of the fish, he had time to think about God's request. He was there for three days before he changed his mind and decided to

[14] https://www.uu.edu/societies/inklings/books/FruitofChristsPresence/Fruit_Chapter2.pdf, pg. 22.
[15] Ibid.

follow God's directive, and he was freed from the large fish. Jonah 1-2; Matthew 12:38-42

How long are you willing to stay trapped? How long are you willing not wanting to face the grief and pain? How long are you not willing to take the steps God has laid out in front of you? How long are you willing not to let go of the pain, the memory? Have you tried to let go?

Reflecting on your fears and grief, what are you going to do about it? Are you ready to be free? Are you ready for peace in your mind and spirit?

Share your thoughts~

Psalm 55:22 (MSG) says,
"Pile your troubles on God's shoulders—he'll carry your load; he'll help you out. He'll never let good people topple into ruin...."

I say to you, "Recognize and acknowledge that you are experiencing some challenges with a mind of peace." List what your challenges are. What are your thoughts, emotions, fears, etc.? Be truthful to yourself! This activity is a step toward your healing.
If you need more space, continue in your self-care journal at the back of this book.

PROVISION

Trauma and Transformation

In John 9:6-7 (NLT), a blind man called out to Jesus, wanting to be healed. But Jesus did not immediately heal him. Jesus first spats on the ground made mud with the saliva and then placed it on the blind man's eyes. Then He told the man to wash his face in the pool of Siloam. Jesus had often been known only to speak a word, and people were healed. However, in this situation, he acted, and the man had to complete an action before he was healed.

In the book of John, chapter 5, a man complained that he couldn't get healed because every time the pool of Bethesda began to stir, everyone beat him to the pool to get healed, and no one would help him. The story is that an angel stirred up the water in the pool, and the first person in the pool was healed. This man could not get help to get to the pool. *I wondered why he never crawled, scooted, or rolled toward the pool. Why didn't someone help him?* His process went on for years until Jesus came by and had a conversation with him. He told him to pick up his bed and walk. And he did.

Know that God sees you drowning in your pain. He sees how you are struggling to receive your healing. He wants to help you. God will send angels (people) to speak to you, assist you, and bring you closer in relationship to Him. When your relationship with God is activated, you will see and experience wonderful miracles.

A Miracle Amid Pain

I had been experiencing excruciating pain in my foot for over two years, beginning in 2019. I would typically take Aleve, lift my feet, and the pain would subside for a time. This time it didn't work. I took prescribed Ibuprofen. It did not work quickly enough. It took three weeks for the pain to subside, compared to three days in the past. I prayed and began to become proactive in my health. I researched to find information that could help me understand why my foot inflamed so frequently. I learned certain foods could trigger it, certain supplements could help reduce it, rubbing ointment and exercising my feet helped. I did not have an inflammation episode for six months. However, when my foot inflamed again, I realized that I was addressing the symptoms and not the cause. I learned that I needed to change doctors and go to a specialist. I found out that it was gout. I learned that everyone's gout triggers are different. Sometimes we spend effort on the symptoms of our problems rather than focusing on our problem. *My miracle: proper diagnosis with proper treatment.*

Some provisions are not immediate and will take time. Just because you did last time does not mean that it will be the same method for success this time. Don't give up! Don't throw in the towel! Be proactive in your transformation. This next story is one transformation that I always find inspiring.

Born in Canada, Michael J. Fox is an award-winning television and film actor whose enduring career as a performer has made him an icon to countless fans worldwide. In 1991, at age 29, he was diagnosed with Parkinson's disease, news he shared with the public in 1998. In 2000, to help advance scientific progress toward a cure for Parkinson's disease, he established The Michael J. Fox Foundation for Parkinson's Research. The disease has advanced in his life and interfered with his ability to perform as an actor, but his efforts have helped many people through his foundation. Michael wasn't healed from the disease, but he pushed forward to make a difference.[16] His transformation happened because he used his platform to gather people financially to help finance the research for this debilitating disease. He was proactive by creating a foundation for intense research, which has helped thousands of individuals with this disease—*his miracle: advanced treatments.*

---

[16] The Michael J Fox Foundation.

Provision is not always immediate. It can be a process. It can be a component of helping others. As with Paul, God did not remove the issue, Paul's "thorn in the flesh," but Paul ministered and healed many people in many countries through the process.

The scriptures and the stories of others helped me process and see God's provision in my own life. For example, in 2007, I was diagnosed with having a left-bundle blockage, and I prayed to be healed many times. I still have the bundle blockage, but my heart condition has not worsened. I realized that I could either be crying over my situation or become proactive. I researched my heart disease, the cause, the symptoms, and the treatment. I realized that I was blessed not to have any severe effects. I took my blood pressure medicine, and I began to make healthier choices. I lost a little weight, and my choices of adding green smoothies and low-impact exercises helped my blood pressure to stay in a healthier range. In 2021, I learned that my heart is flowing normally and is no longer enlarged. Like the man at the healing pool, God may speak to you at times, requiring you to take action instead of sitting and grumbling.

From experience, I know that transformation could be immediate, but being realistic could take a few years. We cannot profess to understand how God works and heals, but I can promise you that each week/month is a step closer to peace of mind if you are willing to do some work. Take the first step.

Take each challenge separately. Don't work on everything at the same time.

The Transformation Process

There are several elements to be aware of in the transformation process:

The Wait – "Meantime"

According to the author and inspirational speaker Iyanla Vanzant, being in the "meantime" means being in a state of limbo.

"When you are not happy where you are, and you are not quite sure if you want to leave or how to leave, you are in the meantime," she explains. "It's a state of limbo. You are hanging on, ready to let go, afraid to fall, not wanting to hurt yourself, afraid you will hurt someone else. In the meantime, you pray the other person will let go first so you will not feel guilty." [17]

I often insert this into my prayers, "In your Scriptures, Lord, your word says in Isaiah 40:31(NIV), 'Those who hope in the LORD will renew their strength. They will soar on wings like

---

[17] Vanzant, Iyanla. In the Meantime: Finding Yourself and the Love You Want. Simon and Schuster, 1999, pages 23-24.

eagles, they will run and not grow weary, they will walk and not be faint.' Lord, I am weak and need strength to move forward. I am exhausted, but I depend on you."

This scripture says you can reach the highest possibility available to you if you wait for the strength of the Lord.

Sleep

Sleep is essential to functioning at your best. The lack of sleep leads to tiredness, weakness, frustration, and it feeds your fears. Also, when you are sleep-deprived, you are a good target for evil thoughts. So, if sleep is a challenge, deal with that first. No rest or lack of sleep affects your mind and body, which challenges your effectiveness in life, work, engaging with others, and so on.

I have found it helpful to insert this scriptural promise into my prayers, "In your Scriptures, Lord, your word says in Matthew 11:28-30(NIV), 'Come to me, all you who are weary and burdened, and I will give you rest. Take my yoke upon you and learn from me, for I am gentle and humble in heart, and you will find rest for your souls.'"

Loneliness

I have learned that I need to interrupt my isolation. I'm an introvert. I love being alone, but my fears feed on my isolation. My ancestors used to say, "An idle mind is the devil's workshop!" Have you isolated yourself? You probably think you're always alone. I did too, but I realized my thoughts and panic attacks became more intense when I was isolated. I needed to get out of the house and see people. By visiting Walmart, a fast-food drive-thru, the park, driving around, going to a movie, or eating at a restaurant, I was able to breathe, feel and see the things God created, like the trees, the breeze, and the sun. Simple human contact – "Hello, how are you", "I'm good, Thank You" can make a world of difference.

Routine

Philippians 4:13(NIV) says, "I can do all this through him who gives me strength."

To aid my process, I decided to create a routine schedule. Getting up with no identifiable purpose or goal was a waste of time in a day and my life. I needed to bring some organization back into my life and not be mentally scattered. I did a soft organization in the rooms of my house. I changed where I sat in a room or sat in another room or outside. I began to set days to work on my nonprofit, relaxation and cleaning the house, etc.

Blessing

I began to think weekly about what good or positive things I had achieved. This process is called encouragement and empowerment. I would think about the hours, minutes, and days, and good moments. Also, I thought about any bad moments I experienced and then how I handled that moment. Then I review how much my reactions to unexpected situations grew. Psalm 29:11(NIV) says, "The Lord gives strength to his people; the Lord blesses his people with peace."

What a blessing! God gives us strength and peace. Whatever journey we are on, he will provide us with strength and peace. I am still on medications for my heart to regulate my blood pressure, but I no longer have those symptoms of faintness and the heart pumping slowly at times. That is a blessing to me.

Know you are blessed in many ways every day. Observe and embrace those daily blessings. It will give you strength and peace each day. There are more scriptures on blessings in chapter six.

Emotion

I went to the Bible daily during my transformation. I would pray and choose a scripture relating to my emotions and challenges. For example, I struggled with *why am I still here?* God sent me to Acts 9:36-43—when the town contacted Peter to bring life back into Tabitha (called Dorcas). The town was sad and pleaded with Peter and shared her character and good works. Dorcas was full of good works and almsdeeds. She was a seamstress. Peter prayed for her, and she rose from death.

Reading this scripture helped me to understand why God may have let me live. I have a servant's heart. I served in my church and community. I helped people, listened to their needs. I knew how to sew, and I did crafts, which I could relate to in Dorcas. No, these individual things were not the specific reasons God saved me, but maybe people who prayed for me shared my character and good works with God. I was significant in authority, but the people I served also prayed for me. The ministers prayed for me. People in my church family prayed for me. I believe the work I had done was pleasing to God. Genesis 33:10(NIV) said, "If I have found favor in your eyes, accept this gift from me. For to see your face is like seeing the face of God now that you have received me favorably."

Fear

2 Timothy 1:7(NIV),

For the Spirit God gave us does not make us timid, but gives us power, love, and self-discipline.

Psalm 34:1-4 (NIV),

I will extol the Lord at all times; his praise will always be on my lips. I will glory in the Lord; let the afflicted hear and rejoice. Glorify the Lord with me; let us exalt his name together. I sought the Lord, and he answered me; he delivered me from all my fears.

My faith was strong, but it was shaken after the trauma. I held on to it the best I could. Fear can bring health issues to the body and mind. You need to starve your sickness by not being fearful all the time. Walk-in faith brings freedom from fear. You must step back out and return to life. It's challenging and scary but obtainable with a little bit of confidence.

Walk out Fear with Faith!

As you know, I was afraid the trauma would repeat, so I would not go outside the house. I used the method below to help me through the process. I also used it in assisting others too afraid to return to life after their trauma experience.

My steps:

- To familiarize myself with society, I went and opened the front door. I stood in the open doorway for a couple of minutes. I stepped back in and closed the door. I went on doing whatever I was doing in the house for a time and then returned to the door. I did this three times a day for a few days.
- Once I felt confident and calm standing in the doorway, I moved to stand on the porch for a few minutes. I would then go back inside the house. I did this three times a day for a few days.
- Once this was conquered, I moved to the car and sat behind the wheel in the driver's seat

with the car door open. I did this a couple of times before I tried it with the car door closed.

- The next step was turning the car on and sitting there with it running for a few minutes. I then placed it in reverse and backed up in the driveway, then put it in drive and moved forward up the driveway. I did this act a couple of times each day for a few days.
- I became comfortable driving in my driveway and decided to take a trip around the neighborhood. You can do this down the street, the block, or around the neighborhood. If you feel comfortable, venture out of the neighborhood.

If you followed the above steps, you have succeeded in getting out of the house and driving. You are working back into living your life. Celebrate this achievement!

One person I assisted with this exercise was fearful of leaving the house. I aided them in realizing that no one was watching them or the house. No cameras or news people were seeking a report. It was safe to go outside.

Romans 8:37 speaks on having victory in your life. I do. So does the person I helped with this exercise.

They are driving again, going out to places, socializing with others again, and enjoying their family. Victory is waiting on you. Claim it! You will have VICTORY!

Maintaining My Faith

Reading of Scriptures and prayers was essential in my healing. The phone calls of a special preacher friend allowing me to share my internal pain and praying for me weekly as I prayed and listened to her were healing conversations. My children were the purpose of my becoming whole again. Family and friends were my encouragement to pursue and persist.

Forgiveness

You must forgive! Others and yourself!

Scripture speaks on forgiveness. It is a command. Through my experience, there were beautiful things that good Christian people said, my friends and family that supported me, and a few church leaders that stayed in touch. Still, many in that group that I have personally helped during their need didn't visit or contact me—that hurt. I held on to anger toward them.

In Job 42:7-17, God told Job to pray for his friends who spoke wrongly of God. Job prayed for them, and God gave him a double blessing: financially and in his family. His actions were an encouragement to my faith, and I prayed for those I believed hurt me. Many didn't know they had hurt me. It did take some time for me to pray for a few people, but I did it. It gave me peace, and that anger diminished.

During this process of learning to forgive, I attended healing classes at Joan Hunter's Ministries, and in one of the sessions, she demonstrated a method of releasing unforgiveness. To my surprise, I used it, and then I used it with someone else. Amazingly, I thought I was going to the healing class for myself and ended up helping others through what I learned.

Unforgiveness brings on illness, stress, pain, and much more. I encourage you to use this technique (explained below) for yourself to cleanse the inner pain from your trauma and hurt and any unforgiveness you are carrying from your time of trauma. I also encourage you to use this technique with others who come to you with inner pain. Speak to the trauma. Speak life back into your body for the healing of your physical body.

Share your thoughts~

Preparation for the Forgiveness Exercise

Who has hurt you? Who are you having a hard time forgiving? Who have you hurt? What wrong have you done, and are you unable to forgive yourself? If any of these resonate with you, you are holding guilt!

Write a list of all those you need to forgive in your life before you continue. Be truthful to yourself! This activity is a step toward your healing. If you need more space, continue in your self-care journal at the back of this book.

Props: Get a box of tissues and a container (trash can) and place it before you.

You can do this exercise with someone or by yourself. After you have completed the exercise, empty the tissues in the outside trash for disposal. Get those rotten emotions out of your home.

Action: Have the person seeking freedom from unforgiveness toward others remove a tissue for each statement (person, sin, event) that you speak. If you are the lead, you hold the box of tissues, and the person takes tissue for each statement they will talk to and place it in your right hand after completing the statement. Why the right hand? In the Bible, power and blessings are in the right hand. (Luke 22:69 and Genesis 48:14)

Symbol: The tissue represents Sin. The right hand represents the cross of Christ. The placing of the tissue in the right hand represents the request for God's forgiveness of the person. (Christ took on the sins of the world and asked God's forgiveness for them while on the cross) Exhibit A.

This exercise separates the sins from the person. Below are statements for various scenarios. You can modify the action of sin and the name of the person but not the words ***italicized***. There is a purpose to those words. Repeat the words in the scenario for each person, sin, etc.

Take a tissue and speak these words. After you complete the statement, place the tissue in the container (trash can) – Exhibit B.

Illustration of the Forgiveness Exercise

Exhibit A: Exercise with Two People

Exhibit B. Exercise Individually

Forgiveness Statements:

1. When someone hurts you:

   Father, _insert the person's name that has hurt you_, is not perfect but has hurt me. And that is sin. I ask you to separate this sin from him/her. I put it on the cross, *(Now put the tissue in the right hand, which represents the cross),* never to be held against him/her again. Father bless him/her. *(Repeat this last phrase three times)*

2. Intimate relationship hurts:

   Father, I gave my heart to ________. It's not his/hers to have anymore. And I take back that part of my heart that I gave to _______. *(Now put the tissues in the right hand, which represents the cross.*) Father, I ask you to heal it. Father, any covenant formed in this relationship, I renounce that covenant, anything bad that came through the covenant, take it from me now, in Jesus' name. Thank you, Jesus. *(Repeat this last phrase three times)*

3. **Other relationship hurts:**

   Father, what _______ did to me was a sin. I felt like I could do nothing right; everything I tried, I failed, and he/she did some things that really hurt, he/she led me on, and all of that is sin. I ask you to separate the sin from him/her and put it on the cross, *(Now put the tissues in the right hand, which represents the cross),* never to be held against him/her again. Father bless him/her. *(Repeat this last phrase three times)*

4. **Your Personal Act of hurt to someone else:**

   Father, what I did was a sin. (The next sentence inserts your sins or the name of the person/people) I _________________________. I ask you to separate the sin from me and put it on the cross *(Now put the tissues in the right hand, representing the cross)* never to be held against me again. Father bless me. *(Repeat this last phrase three times)*

My Transformation: Miracle

I survived my trauma with a purpose. I know God loves me, and I trust Him daily. It is wonderful to help people through their trauma and pain to move toward receiving their joy again. They learn that they can live life again without or with little fear.

My life began to prosper. I am not speaking of only finances but spiritually and in service. My non-profit, Babies Youth Children Empowerment Ministries, Inc. (www.byceministries.org), has assisted many students diagnosed with learning disabilities and those with undiagnosed learning challenges in becoming successful in school. Through our programs, we increased their self-esteem and instilled unique learning styles to aid in their academic success - Help families help their students.

God led me to begin a worship ministry, adding nursing homes to my already established summer vacation Bible camps. I am the pastor to the unchurched performing funerals, weddings, speaking, preaching, and more. I earned a Doctor in Ministry. I began an online T-Shirt and accessory business with inspirational and affirmational quotes. I am an author!

(http://www.livingmydestiny2020.com)

I never saw these accomplishments being a part of my journey, but I am blessed and grateful that they are. I am glad I went through the transformation process. To God be the glory!

When you begin your transformation, you are allowing God to expand your territory or accomplishments and success. Don't give up!

To guarantee my victory, reading scriptures and praying were a necessity. The following few chapters will provide you with tools to aid you through your transformation.

Let's pray.

> *"God, I'm tired of dragging this heavy load around with me. I'm ready to let it go so I can get on with my life and experience a closer relationship with You. Help me to remember that whatever You tell me to do, You will give me the ability to do it, and You always love me and have my best interest at heart. I trust You, Lord, to work everything out for my good."*
>
> *~ Joyce Meyer* [18]

As a follower of Jesus Christ, I would be remiss if

---

[18] Joyce Meyer Ministries, Keep Your Eye on the Prize.

I did not address your spiritual relationship. When you journey through the process of transformation, I pray your relationship with God increases.

If you don't have a relationship and want one, this is God's commitment in Romans 10:8-10 (NIV). It says, *"The word is near you; it is in your mouth and in your heart, that is, the message concerning faith that we proclaim. If you declare with your mouth, Jesus is Lord, and believe in your heart that God raised him from the dead, you will be saved. For it is with your heart that you believe and are justified, and it is with your mouth that you profess your faith and are saved." Verse 17 – "Consequently, faith comes from hearing the message, and the message is heard through the word about Christ."* I personally say to you, find a good bible study or teaching church so that you can study and learn the word about Christ (gospel).

Chapter Five

PRAYING THE SCRIPTURES

"What more do I have to do to let you know that I've got you?" ~God

God spoke the above statement in my spirit during my time of continuous fear and questioning of God. It was a powerful statement. God was letting me know that he loves me, will protect me, will provide for me, will be with me, and that he has me in his powerful hands. It was a word of strengthening my trust. I could have died, or my body could have been permanently damaged, but none of that happened. When you look at me, I am alive, and there is no physical and no mental evidence of what I experienced during that trauma. I praise God for that. I share my story of how good God was to me at every opportunity.

Psalm 119:11(ESV),

"You shall therefore lay up these words of mine in your heart and in your soul, and you shall bind them as a sign on your hand, and they shall be as frontlets between your eyes."

There are several scriptures that I hold dear to my heart. I may not remember the book, chapter, and verse at the time, but I know the words and can find them when I need them. The memory of those scriptures has aided me in making it through many rough days. Write down scriptures that encourage you in your self-care journal at the back of this book.

The Model Prayer

Searching for the spiritual significance of numbers was the beginning of my determination to heal from the inside, spiritually and mentally. To heal from the inside, you must deal with the spirit within you. I began to pray and search the scriptures that addressed my emotions, and I prayed daily on those scriptures for healing from those negative emotions.

I was desperate for change, and I began

remembering some of the Biblical characters' prayers or ways they approached God for their needs.

Jacob decided to grab the angel's leg saying he would not let go until he blessed him. Genesis 32:22-31

Hezekiah turned to the wall while lying in his bed and prayed to God after receiving the message that he would die. God heard and gave him fifteen more years. 2 Kings 20:1-6

Jesus gave a model of a prayer to the disciples when they inquired about how to pray. Many of us learned it as a child. Matthew 6:9-13 (CSB) says,

"Therefore, you should pray like this:

Our Father in heaven,
Your name be honored as holy.
Your Kingdom come.
Your will be done on earth as it is in heaven.
Give us today our daily bread.
And forgive us our debts, as we also have forgiven our debtors.
And do not bring us into temptation but deliver us from the evil one.
[For Yours is the Kingdom and the power
and the glory forever. Amen.]

Understanding the Model Prayer

Let's look at The Lord's Prayer more closely. In this model of prayer, Jesus explained how we should approach God when we are ready to converse with him through prayer. It is helpful to understand the purpose of the words.

"Our Father (who art) in heaven" (v. 9) **acknowledges God's Paternity.** Through this, we recognize our relationship with God, who is our Provider and Protector. We also recognize that God rules from Heaven and is in control (Psalm 11:4; Hebrews 12:9). Therefore, submit to Him and live under a covenant!

"Hallowed be your name" (v. 9) **acknowledges God's Person.** God is Holy and must be acknowledged by man as Holy (Psalm 111:9).

"Your kingdom come" (v.10) **acknowledges God's Program.** Kingdom recognizes God's Sovereignty, Royal Power, and Rule.

"Your will be done on earth as it is in heaven" (v.10) **acknowledges God's Purposes.** We must understand that God's Will has priority over our will – His purpose for us!

"Give us this day our daily bread" (v.11) **acknowledges God's Provisions.** We must rely on God each day! He is our Provider.

"And forgive us our debts, as we forgive our debtors" (v.12) **acknowledges God's Pardon.** God forgives us just as we forgive others. We need forgiveness, and when we confess our sins to Him, He forgives! If we cannot/will not forgive, we won't be forgiven—Matthew 6:14-15 and 7:2.

"And do not lead us into temptation, But deliver us from the evil one" (v.13) **acknowledges God's Protection.** We need to pray, not be led into temptation. Ask God to "Help us not to be led into temptation" (to not succumb to temptation) and give us a way of escape (through faith).

"For yours is the Kingdom and the power and the glory forever. Amen" (v.13) **acknowledges God's Preeminence and Praise;** giving Praise to God and saying Amen: "So it is, so be it, may it be fulfilled." [19]

---

[19] http://bibleanswer.com/modelpra.html

I pray that the above explanation helps you understand what Jesus taught us in how to communicate with God through prayer.

Prayer and Fasting

Prayer is a powerful tool and will change your life when you put it into practice. When done in combination with fasting, it will be even more powerful, with more breakthroughs. There are specific scenarios where the partnership of prayer and fasting is required. There are many reasons to fast.

For example, I prayed for a friend who was in ICU for weeks. They were reintroducing them to swallowing food to remove their feeding tube. God instructed me not to eat for three hours and pray on this scripture. I reached out to the family, and they agreed and invited others to participate. They were able to swallow the next day. I believe being obedient and fasting in agreement brought about victory. (This prayer is on page 122)

You must understand, some prayers require intense sacrifice during spiritual warfare. This means when there is no explanation for the trauma experience, it may be a spiritual attack on one's life. This book is not a Bible study, but I suggest you read about spiritual warfare – Satan attacks our assignment, destiny, purpose, etc.

Fasting can be approached with many methods. Some individuals do all liquids (water, natural juices) fast; a Daniel fast involves cutting out meat and eating only fruits and vegetables. Intermittent fasting is another option, or you could do a focused fast by removing certain foods or activities. The length of your fast is entirely between you and God. Some do days or weeks. Some fast by hours in a day, for example, 6 am – 6 pm, or 9 am – 3 pm.

Scriptures on Fasting

Daniel 9:3 (NIV),

So I turned to the Lord God and pleaded with him in prayer and petition, in **fasting.**

Matthew 4:2(NIV),

After **fasting** for forty days and forty nights, he was hungry.

Matthew 6:16(NIV),

"When you fast, do not look somber as the hypocrites do, for they disfigure their faces to show others they are **fasting**. Truly I tell you, they have received their reward in full.

Luke 2:37(NIV),
There was a widow until she was eighty-four. She never left the temple but worshiped night and day, **fasting** and praying.

Ephesians 6:12(NIV) says, "For our struggle is not against flesh and blood, but against the rulers, against the authorities, against the powers of this dark world and against the spiritual forces of evil in the heavenly realms."

Fasting helps you focus on the more important things in life. In my own life, I have found that when I fast with prayer, I hear God's voice and see his guidance more clearly. For example, I fasted to understand what I was supposed to do about my ordination. That wonderful Sunday, the visiting preacher confirmed this, saying God was sending me a different way to obtain my ordination. I was ordained through a ministry with an established program and reputation helping those called to ministry who don't have access to a church institution.

Scriptural Prayer

In desperate moments, I began prayers like this:

Father, God Almighty, my creator, provider, protector, You are awesome, a wonderful counselor, and a forgiving God. I approach You in worship and need. In my greatest need, I come to Your throne boldly as Your Word says in Hebrews 4:16(NIV), "Let us then approach God's throne of grace with confidence, so that we may receive mercy and find grace to help us in our time of need."

Jesus, the Son of God, thank You for Your sacrifice so that I may have a personal relationship with God. As the Word says, Romans 8:34(NIV), "Who then is the one who condemns? No one. Christ Jesus who died—more than that, who was raised to life—is at the right hand of God and is also interceding for us." Jesus, please plea to God on my behalf to forgive me of my sins (wrongness), those known and unknown. I try hard to do right. I try hard to forgive those who have done me wrong and not to hold any grudges.

Holy Spirit, my comforter, wisdom guide, and wise counsel, I ask would You interpret to God on my behalf what I am trying to say when it is apparent that I am not adequate in my presentation. The Word says in Romans 8:26(NIV) that "the Spirit helps us in our weakness. We do not know what we ought to pray for, but the Spirit Himself intercedes for us through wordless groans." I have so much heaviness and stress that I may not say it gracefully or respectfully, so I need You to interpret what I am saying to the Father.

God, I thank You for creating me and loving me even when I am unlovable. I have not been the perfect child, but You continue to love and bless my family and me. I am grateful. I thank You for hearing my plea. God, I am quoting the Word to You because You said that your Word would not return void. In Your Word, Isaiah 55:11(NIV) says, "So is My Word that goes out from my mouth: It will not return to me empty but will accomplish what I desire and achieve the purpose for which I sent it."

I am a scriptural person of prayer. I find scriptures related to the need and speak the words out, as I included them in my prayer above.

When I pray, I often insert Isaiah 55:11 into my prayers, as I did in the prayer above. God's Word promises that His Word will not return to Him empty. Let us speak His Word!

I am sharing with you some of the scriptural prayers that worked for me. They gave me peace. Through quoting promises in Scripture, I prayed for others in need—in this, I found a sense of purpose. I pray and believe that they will work for you if you believe. You can modify them to your situation.

God, I pray this prayer in thanksgiving, knowing and believing that You have heard me. I thank You for responding to my request. I believe You know all, and You were aware that this would be my fate. I believe You allowed this to happen, and I thank You for keeping me in my right mind.

Praying pretty prayers won't always bring us comfort, especially when overwhelmed or anxious about a situation. I am not always in a posture of prayer. There were times when I prayed to God earnestly, and He remained silent. It was then that I elevated my prayers by:

- Quoting Jacob when he struggled with the angel, or
- Referencing Hezekiah's praying to God, the answer to his prayers was 15 additional years of life.
- I may add how God protected Daniel when he was in the den of lions by closing their mouths; or
- The three Hebrew boys, Shadrach, Meshach, and Abednego, in the fiery furnace and how

the Holy Spirit stepped into the midst of their situation.

My Prayers Spoken on Healing

Here are some prayer bits created in my heart:

(A)God, I need You. My mind is destroying me just as Paul spoke in 2 Corinthians 12:9 that Satan's witnesses haunted him. They are haunting me now. I am afraid and frustrated. (B) As Jacob said, "I'm not going to let You go until You bless me." I'm saying, "God, I'm going to keep praying for ____ until You bless me, heal me, speak to me about... (Whatever my needs were)". (C) I believe You are a healer as Your Word says in Psalm 103 that You are a healer of all disease. (D) I believe your Word and trust You because You said Your Word does not return to You void (Isaiah 55:11).
In Jesus' name, Amen.

At one time, God prompted me to call sister preachers to form a group of prayer warriors to pray for a child experiencing multiple surgeries, and the doctors did not know the cause. Many people prayed. God guided us to pray every six hours (6 am, 12 noon, 6 pm, and 12 midnight), which would aid in the child's healing. A scripture was chosen to be read at each session. These were God's instructions to me, and I shared with the individuals I asked to pray with me.

We were to pray weekly, one healing scripture three times a day until his healing appeared. The number three means divine completeness and perfection; reflect the Trinity (the Father, Son, and the Holy Spirit); and Jesus was tempted three times in the wilderness. These scriptures on threes support the instructions I received:

1 Kings 17:21-22 (NIV),

Then he stretched himself out on the boy three times and cried out to the Lord, "Lord my God, let this boy's life return to him!" The Lord heard Elijah's cry, and the boy's life returned to him, and he lived.

Matthew 12:40(NIV),

For as Jonah was three days and three nights in the belly of a huge fish, so the Son of Man will be three days and three nights in the heart of the earth.

Mark 9:31 (NIV),

Because he was teaching his disciples, he said to

them, "The Son of Man is going to be delivered into the hands of men. They will kill him, and after three days he will rise."

Daniel 6:10 (NIV),

Now when Daniel learned that the decree had been published, he went home to his upstairs room where the windows opened toward Jerusalem. Three times a day he got down on his knees and prayed, giving thanks to his God, just as he had done before.

Prayers for a Child

The sister preachers and I prayed on these scriptures daily for complete supernatural healing and restoration and that he would not have any residual from his illness.

Acts 9:38-39 (MSG),

Some of the disciples had heard that Peter was visiting in nearby Lydda and sent two men to ask if he would be so kind as to come over. Peter got right up and went with them. They took him into the room where Tabitha's body was laid out. Her old friends, most of them widows, were in the room mourning. They showed Peter pieces of clothing the

Gazelle had made while she was with them. Peter put the widows all out of the room. He knelt and prayed. Then he spoke directly to the body: "Tabitha, get up."

Acts 10:9(NIV) says, "About noon the following day as they were on their journey and approaching the city, Peter went up on the roof to pray."

Acts 12:5(NIV) says, "So Peter was kept in prison, but the church was earnestly praying to God for him."

Isaiah 55:11(NIV) says, "So is my word that goes out from my mouth: It will not return to me empty, but will accomplish what I desire and achieve the purpose for which I sent it."

Matthew 8:14-15(NIV) says, "When Jesus came into Peter's house, he saw Peter's mother-in-law lying in bed with a fever. 15 He touched her hand and the fever left her, and she got up and began to wait on him."

James 5:13-16(NIV), a prayer of faith, says, "Is anyone among you in trouble? Let them pray. Is anyone happy? Let them sing songs of praise. Is anyone among you sick? Let them call the elders of the church to pray over them and anoint them with oil in the name of the Lord. And the prayer offered in faith will make the sick person well; the Lord will raise them up. If they have sinned, they will be forgiven. Therefore, confess your sins to each other and pray for each other so that you may be healed. The prayer of a righteous person is powerful and effective."

Acts 28:8(NIV) says, "His father was sick in bed, suffering from fever and dysentery. Paul went in to see him and, after prayer, placed his hands on him and healed him."

Psalm 103:1-3(NIV) says, "Praise the Lord, my soul; all my inmost being, praise his holy name. Praise the Lord, my soul, and forget not all his benefits—who forgives all your sins and heals all your diseases."

Good News – After several surgeries, the child's issue ceased, and the child's health was restored.

Prayers for a friend in ICU

Father God, we thank You for creating and loving us. We thank You, Jesus, for Your sacrifice, receiving and enduring the pain of crucifixion for our salvation and eternal life.

Our wife, mother, sister, ______, is enduring pain, discomfort, stress, and many other emotions because of this journey she has been assigned. We know that many have taken this journey before her with victory. We believe in the scriptures. We trust in Your Word. Psalm 121:1-2 NIV says, "I lift up my eyes to the mountains—where does my help come from? My help comes from the Lord, the Maker of heaven and earth." Believing Your Word does not return void, we speak this scripture. She needs Your help.
In Jesus' Name, Amen.

We are still looking to You, Father, for Your help on her behalf. Jesus, please continue to intercede and plead ____ case before the Father. (Romans 8:34) Holy Spirit speak to the Father, interpreting our words into his language. (Romans 8:26-27) We are forever grateful. Father, You are our first resource of provision. Grant the medical team and family wisdom towards excellent care. We are thankful for her progress, and we give You praise for Your responses. We continually give You praise. In Jesus' Name, Amen.

Father, we profess Your Word and stand on Your promises. In Your Word, Psalm 29:11 (NIV), it says, "Who then is the one who condemns? No one. Christ Jesus who died—more than that, who was raised to life—is at the right hand of God and is also interceding for us." Psalm 28:7-8 (NIV) says, "The

Lord is my strength and my shield; my heart trusts in him, and he helps me. My heart leaps for joy, and with my song, I praise him. The Lord is the strength of his people, a fortress of salvation for his anointed one." Lord _____ needs Your healing Spirit. We stand on these scriptures believing in Your healing power. Isaiah 35:3-4 (MSG) says, "Energize the limp hands, strengthen the rubbery knees. Tell fearful souls, "Courage! Take heart! GOD is here, right here, on his way to put things right and redress all wrongs. He's on his way! He'll save you!" In Jeremiah 30:17 (NIV), "But I will restore you to health and heal your wounds,' declares the Lord, 'because you are called an outcast, Zion for whom no one cares.'" Yes, Lord, please save ______. In Jesus' Name, Amen.

Father, hear our prayer again. We know that You continue to supply all her needs. Comfort her with Your words and presence. Calm her fears as Jesus spoke to the storm, peace is still, and the storms obeyed. Remind her Father of Your comment in Philippians 4:13 (NIV); "I can do all this through him who gives me strength." Thank You, Jesus, for Your healing power. Thank You, Jesus, for Your strength.
Thank You, Jesus, for sacrificing for us.
In Jesus' Name, Amen.

Prayer for digestion for a friend

There are times we must be bold before the throne of God. In this particular scenario, God said, don't (those praying) eat for three hours, and we prayed this prayer. We prayed on these things until God responded. The medical staff decided to test my friend to receiving food, and there were three hours left.

Father, we pray that her body receives the food and processes the food naturally as designed. Her digestive system functions as God created. Her reflux is healed. The muscles (sphincter) function properly. Matthew 15:17 (NIV) says, "Don't you see that whatever enters the mouth goes into the stomach and then out of the body?" Mark 7:18-19 (NIV), says "'Are you so dull?' he asked. 'Don't you see that nothing that enters a person from the outside can defile them? For it doesn't go into their heart but into their stomach, and then out of the body.'" (In saying this, Jesus declared all foods clean.) I pray for forgiveness on her behalf. In Jesus' Name, Amen.

Scriptures that relate to digestion:

Matthew 15:17(NIV), "Don't you see that whatever enters the mouth goes into the stomach and then out of the body?

2 Samuel 16:1-2(NIV),
When David had gone a short distance beyond the summit, there was Ziba, the steward of Mephibosheth, waiting to meet him. He had a string of donkeys saddled and loaded with two hundred loaves of bread, a hundred cakes of raisins, a hundred cakes of figs and a skin of wine. The king asked Ziba, "Why have you brought these?" Ziba answered, "The donkeys are for the king's household to ride on, the bread and fruit are for the men to eat, and the wine is to refresh those who become exhausted in the wilderness."

3 John 2(NIV),
Dear friend, I pray that you may enjoy good health and that all may go well with you, even as your soul is getting along well.

Prayers for Breathing Issues (COVID)

These scriptures addressed breathing issues and other internal health challenges. I spoke these prayers on behalf of those with health challenges, including those related to the Covid-19 virus, but not limited to Covid-19. This virus has harmed many families. Many in ICU were on their death beds and ventilators. Some individuals have had a severe effect on their health after recovery from the virus.

Many individuals have died. I knew friends who were affected by the virus. Some recovered, and a few died. I felt in my heart to pray for those in ICU affected by Covid-19.

Prayer examples,

Father, God Almighty, You are our provider, protector, and creator. You know us better than anyone else. This virus is affecting many of Your children, and many are dying. I ask in the name of Jesus that Your restoration of Lazurus can happen to ______. Your Word says in John 11:43 (NIV), "When he had said this, Jesus called in a loud voice, 'Lazarus, come out!'" John 12:1-3 (NIV) says, "Six days before the Passover, Jesus came to Bethany, where Lazarus lived, whom Jesus had raised from the dead. Here a dinner was given in Jesus' honor. Martha served while Lazarus was among those reclining at the table with him. Then Mary took about a pint of pure nard, an expensive perfume; she poured it on Jesus' feet and wiped his feet with her hair. And the house was filled with the fragrance of the perfume." We will be forever grateful for Your healing of ______. We pray that You speak to them while they are in ICU and let them know You are there with them. We bless Your name. We worship You. We'll give to those in need as You guide us. In Jesus' Name, Amen.

Father God, Our Creator, Our Healer, Your Word says in Psalm 103 that You are the healer of all diseases; Psalm 55 speaks on Your Word not returning Void. I pray in faith on Your Word, Father in Heaven. Whatever we ask in Jesus' name, it shall be done according to Your will according to John 14:13, "And whatsoever ye shall ask in my name, that will I do, that the Father may be glorified in the Son." I come before You humbly at Your throne of mercy, I ask Jesus to intercede to the Father upon ______ behalf, and I seek the Holy Spirit to interpret to the Father my plea where my words are inadequate. I pray that You supernaturally heal ______. His/Her body is weak and weary. You are the creator of our bodies, and You know how it operates. I ask that You heal his/her body by strengthening his/her kidneys and lungs. And any other organ affected by Covid. We took our first breath because You breathed into our nostrils and gave us life. I ask that You be the breath of ______ lungs and body so that they may be revived in Jesus' name. Father, I ask that You supernaturally perform a transfusion of Jesus' blood into _____ body so that it may rejuvenate his/her blood cells to fight the virus in her body. God of Lazarus, I ask that You raise his/her body from the grave of sickness and give it life. Prepare his/her body to receive the meat, fruits, and water of this earth that You created. In Jesus' name, Amen.

Father God, You healed the body of Job, and I know You can raise his/her body in good health. Regulate his/her body, his/her vital sign to normalcy. Give him/her a clear mind. Whisper to him/her that You are there, and he/she should mount up on wings like an eagle. God, ______ needs You, and I desire Your will. Your Word says You would give us our heart's desires. I lay my request before Your throne of mercy. I ask for forgiveness for not being all that I should be. I thank You, God, for hearing my plea. I thank You, Jesus, for interceding for _____. I thank You, Holy Spirit, for interpreting these words to the Father upon my behalf. All these things I ask in Jesus' name, Amen.

Chapter Six

SCRIPTURES: AFFIRMATION

Sometimes you need more people praying with and for you during spiritual warfare or against strongholds in your situation.

Below, I included scriptures I spoke out weekly and sometimes daily during my transformation. Do this process, however long you need to affirm God's word and believe his word. I would choose one scripture and read it daily until I felt peace and strength. I would start with the statement, *"Lord, Isaiah 55:11 says that Your Word would not return void. I am reading Your Word to You, and I pray for Your healing power, guidance, comfort, and peace. I am wrestling right now, and I need your peace."*

Search for scriptures relating to your emotions and situations. You can use the internet and type how you feel, adding "biblical" or "spiritual" to your search. Use a concordance to find scriptures in the

Bible. Use Bible commentaries if you don't understand what it is saying. And remember always to pray.

All scriptures below are quotes from the New International Version (NIV) except where noted.

Remain Calm!

Philippians 4:6-7,

Do not be anxious about anything, but in every situation, by prayer and petition, with thanksgiving, present your requests to God. And the peace of God, which transcends all understanding, will guard your hearts and your minds in Christ Jesus.

Matthew 8:23-27,

Then he got into the boat, and his disciples followed him. Suddenly, a furious storm came up on the lake so that the waves swept over the boat. But Jesus was sleeping. The disciples went and woke him, saying, "Lord, save us! We're going to drown!" He replied, "You of little faith, why are you so afraid?" Then he got up and rebuked the winds and the waves, and it was completely calm. The men were amazed and asked, "What kind of man is this? Even the winds and the waves obey him!"

Psalm 103,

Praise the Lord, my soul; all my inmost being, praise his holy name. Praise the Lord, my soul, and forget not all his benefits—who forgives all your sins and heals all your diseases, who redeems your life from the pit and crowns you with love and compassion, who satisfies your desires with good things so that your youth is renewed like the eagle's.

Psalm 17:8,

Keep me as the apple of your eye; hide me in the shadow of your wings.

Be Confident in the Promises of God!

2 Thessalonians 1:5-6,

All this is evidence that God's judgment is right, and as a result, you will be counted worthy of the kingdom of God, for which you are suffering. God is just: He will pay back trouble to those who trouble you and give relief to you who are troubled and to us as well. This will happen when the Lord Jesus is revealed from heaven in blazing fire with his powerful angels.

Proverbs 4:20-23,

My son, pay attention to what I say; turn your ear to my words. Do not let them out of your sight; keep them within your heart, for they are life to those who find them and health to one's whole body. Above all else, guard your heart, for everything you do flows from it.

Isaiah 43:19,

See, I am doing a new thing! Now it springs up; do you not perceive it? I am making a way in the wilderness and streams in the wasteland.

2 Corinthians 12: 7-9,

Therefore, in order to keep me from becoming conceited, I was given a thorn in my flesh, a messenger of Satan, to torment me. Three times I pleaded with the Lord to take it away from me. But he said to me, "My grace is sufficient for you, for my power is made perfect in weakness." Therefore, I will boast all the more gladly about my weaknesses, so that Christ's power may rest on me.

Philippians 4:13,

I can do all things through Christ who strengthens me.

The Shift – Alignment!

Genesis 12:1-4,

The Lord had said to Abram, "Go from your country, your people and your father's household to the land I will show you. "I will make you into a great nation, and I will bless you; I will make your name great, and you will be a blessing. I will bless those who bless you, and whoever curses you I will curse, and all peoples on earth will be blessed through you." So, Abram went, as the Lord had told him; and Lot went with him. Abram was seventy-five years old when he set out from Harran.

2 Corinthians 10:3-5,

For though we live in the world, we do not wage war as the world does. The weapons we fight with are not the weapons of the world. On the contrary, they have divine power to demolish strongholds. We demolish arguments and every pretension that sets itself up against the knowledge of God, and we take captive every thought to make it obedient to Christ.

Be Strong!

2 Timothy 1:7,

For the Spirit God gave us does not make us timid, but gives us power, love, and self-discipline.

Ephesians 3:20,

Now to him who is able to do immeasurably more than all we ask or imagine, according to his power that is at work within us.

Philippians 4:19,

And my God will meet all your needs according to the riches of his glory in Christ Jesus.

John 14:26,

But the Advocate, the Holy Spirit, whom the Father will send in my name, will teach you all things and will remind you of everything I have said to you.

Acts 12:5-7,

So, Peter was kept in prison, but the church was earnestly praying to God for him. The night before Herod was to bring him to trial, Peter was sleeping between two soldiers, bound with two chains, and sentries stood guard at the entrance. Suddenly an angel of the Lord appeared, and a light shone in the cell. He struck Peter on the side and woke him up. "Quick, get up!" he said, and the chains fell off Peter's wrists.

Your Actions!

James 5:12,

Above all, my brothers and sisters, do not swear—not by heaven or by earth or by anything else. All you need to say is a simple "Yes" or "No." Otherwise you will be condemned.

Proverbs 16:9,

In their hearts, humans plan their course, but the Lord establishes their steps.

Proverbs 3:5-12,

Trust in the Lord with all your heart and lean not on your own understanding; in all your ways, submit to him, and he will make your paths straight. Do not be wise in your own eyes; fear the Lord and shun evil. This will bring health to your body and nourishment to your bones.

John 14:1,

Do not let your hearts be troubled. You believe in God; believe also in me.

Psalm 55:16-18, 22

As for me, I call to God, and the Lord saves me.
Evening, morning, and noon I cry out in distress,
and he hears my voice. He rescues me unharmed
from the battle waged against me, even though
many oppose me. Cast your cares on the Lord, and

he will sustain you; He will never let the righteous be shaken.

Chapter Seven

MORE TRIUMPHANT VICTORIES

Nick Vujicic ("voo-yi-chich")

An Australian-American born without arms or legs has become a world-renowned speaker, New York Times best-selling author, life coach, and entrepreneur.

Nick faced tremendous obstacles in life—from living life without limbs to being bullied at school and fearful for his future with no purpose in sight. Without hope, his feelings of helplessness and isolation led him to attempt suicide. Nick persevered through life's challenges and discovered key principles which enabled him to find his purpose and turn obstacles into opportunities, making him one of the most sought-after keynote speakers in the world! Millions of people have found hope, purpose, and the strength to overcome their challenges through Nick's inspirational speeches and powerful coaching. He is married and has children. [20]

Tracy Morgan

Tracy was among those riding in a rented minibus after a stop on a comedy tour in Dover, Delaware, when it was struck from behind by a semi-truck, causing a massive chain-reaction collision. Morgan had to be airlifted to a hospital in New Jersey, where he was treated for numerous serious injuries and head trauma, after which he needed to undergo months of physical therapy and rehabilitation. "I thank GOD for my family. I am eternally grateful for the love and support they give me. My wife, daughter, sons, and friends are what got me back on my feet," Morgan continued in his contemplative series of Twitter posts. "I live every day trying to do right by them and make the most of this second chance." He is acting again. [21]

---

[20] www.Nick Vujicic.com

[21] https://www.yahoo.com/entertainment/tracy-morgan-shares-emotional-message-023858087.html

Sharon Stone

Sharon revealed the impact her 2001 health crisis had on her career. The Academy Award-nominated actress opened up about her massive stroke and "nine-day brain bleed" at an event for the Women's Brain Health Initiative. Stone estimated it took "about seven years" following her stroke to heal. The "Casino" star said she experienced blows to her personal life and career. "(From) trying to keep custody of my son to just functioning—to be able to work at all," she remembered. "I was so grateful to Bernard Arnault (Chairman and CEO of LVMH), who rescued me by giving me a Dior contract. But I had to remortgage my house. I lost everything I had." "I lost my place in the business. I was like the hottest movie star, you know?" she continued. "It was like Miss Princess Diana and me; we were so famous—and she died, and I had a stroke. And we were forgotten."

"I didn't get to the hospital until day three or four of my stroke. Most people die," she said. "I had a 1% chance of living by the time I got surgery—and they wouldn't know for a month if I would live." But the 61-year-old continues to thrive.[22]

---

[22]https://www.usatoday.com/story/entertainment/celebrities/2019/07/19/sharon-stone-stroke-impaled-her-career-i-lost-everything/1776056001/

Finding My Miracle Amid Pain

Everyone will have an encouraging story to share with others. I have had many traumas in my life, but this one trauma in 2011 paved the road to my sharing my story with you.

Now in my sixties, I am still doing great works for the Lord. My story is not over. I have learned that when I open my eyes each morning, there's a purpose for me that day. When I have a challenging day, I sometimes still fall into emotional eating, but far less frequently than before, and many times with healthy treats because I still want to be healthy. As I age, I am experiencing new health challenges, but I am proactive in my care and healing. There are so many resources on the internet for guidance. The internet is not my doctor, but it gives me information to discuss with my doctor.

I shared this earlier, but I want to highlight it again. I am an ordained minister. That 2011 trauma only delayed my ordination; it didn't stop it. I am a pastor of Nursing Home Worship Services and Summer Youth Bible Camps in underserved communities. I am the founder and Executive

Director of a non-profit that nurtures students with learning disabilities and challenges, teaching them to succeed academically and with life skills. I am leaving a legacy for my family through business ventures. I am an author. I am still moving and making myself available for good works as a servant of God. I was blessed to travel to Cape Town, London, and Hong Kong through my Doctor in Ministry program in my sixties. That travel was the icing on my cake. I experienced knee issues in London, back issues in Cape Town because of the long hours of air travel, and high blood pressure in Hong Kong, but I made it through each trip. My cohorts and seminary leaders were terrific. They were caring and supportive of me.

I am full of hope and joy. I talk to God every day – not necessarily in prayer form. The most significant victory was witnessing my oldest grandson graduate from high school and college and my youngest daughter graduate from college. God gave me the desires of my heart. I am excited about my future. Living My Destiny! (www.livingmydestiny2020.com)

Don't give up! Every time your eyes open, you have a purpose for that day. Challenging days strengthen and encourage you for victory. There is a saying that setbacks set you up for a comeback. Remember that it's not over until God says it is! So, find your miracles! List them in the self-care journal.

YOUR SELF-CARE JOURNAL

The journal provides support for your exercises throughout the book. If you need additional space, these pages will be the source for your writing needs. If you have inspiration from reading, you can document it here. If you have a prayer, Scriptures, or quotes you want to record, do it here. If you have additional comments or questions, you can write them here. Whatever thoughts you need to capture, do it here in your journal.

Each page of the journal has a short line designed as your index. You can capture the chapter and page relating to your comments. Or you can give the page a title. These journal pages are yours to use in whichever way you feel led.

Your Self-Care Journal

Your Self-Care Journal

Your Self-Care Journal

Your Self-Care Journal

Your Self-Care Journal

Your Self-Care Journal

Your Self-Care Journal

Your Self-Care Journal

Your Self-Care Journal

Your Self-Care Journal

Your Self-Care Journal

About the Author

Reverend Dr. Lynda Wright Gittens is an individual with compassion and love for God and his people (some require more God strength). She is an ordained minister of the Gospel and ministers to young people and adults. Dr. Lynda earned a Master of Divinity at the age of 58 and a Doctor in Ministry in Leadership at the age of 65. She is a founder of the non-profit Babies Youth Children Empowerment Ministries, an entrepreneur (Living My Destiny, Event Planner), and author. She retired after 33 years as a tax accountant and 40 years as a Volunteer in the community yet continues to serve the community because her purpose is serving and pleasing God.

A *Jesus Follower, Faith-Walker, Prayer Warrior, Overcomer, Encourager, Missionary, Preacher, Speaker, Mother, Sister, Aunt, Friend, Entrepreneur, Victorious Survivor, Teacher, Curriculum Developer and Leader of seminars and conferences.*

Printed in Great Britain
by Amazon

68628720R00112